VGM Opportunities S

OPPORTUNITIES IN COMPUTER SYSTEMS CAREERS (SOFTWARE)

Julie Kling Burns

Foreword by
George R. Eggert, CSP
Executive Director
Institute for Certification of Computer Professionals

VGM Career Horizons
a division of *NTC Publishing Group*
Lincolnwood, Illinois USA

To the men and women beginning
their careers in the field.

Cover Photo Credits:
Upper left courtesy of Intel Corporation; upper right, lower right, and lower left courtesy of International Business Machines Corporation.

Library of Congress Cataloging-in-Publication Data

Burns, Julie.
    Opportunities in computer systems careers / Julie Kling Burns ; foreword by George R. Eggert.
      p. cm.
    Includes bibliographical references.
    ISBN 0-8442-4598-4 (h : alk. paper). — ISBN 0-8442-4599-2 (p : alk. paper)
    1. Electronic data processing—Vocational guidance. 2. Computer science—Vocational guidance   I. Title
QA76.25.B87   1996
004'.023—dc20   96-5971
                                                                                  CIP

1997 Printing

Published by VGM Career Horizons, a division of NTC Publishing Group
4255 West Touhy Avenue
Lincolnwood (Chicago), Illinois 60646-1975, U.S.A.
© 1996 by NTC Publishing Group. All rights reserved.
No part of this book may be reproduced, stored in a retrieval
system, or transmitted in any form or by any means,
electronic, mechanical, photocopying, recording or otherwise,
without the prior permission of NTC Publishing Group.
Manufactured in the United States of America.

7 8 9 0 VP 9 8 7 6 5 4 3 2

CONTENTS

About the Author v
Foreword vii
Introduction.. ix

1. **A Look at Computers and Computer Careers** 1

   A brief history of computers. Where do computer professionals work? Hardware and software professionals. Types of employers. Is a job in computer software for you?

2. **Working Inside the Computer Industry** 16

   Hardware and product development. Software product development. Developing shrink-wrap and commercial software. Research and development (R&D). Working for a start-up. Marketing and sales.

3. **Working for Everyone Else**............................38

   Employers and environments. Corporate software development. Systems analysis. EDP auditor. Operations. Information systems departments. Systems integrators, VARs, and consultants. Going independent.

4. **Five Career Profiles**.................................57

   Operating systems programmer. Engineering programmer, hardware design team. Applications programmer, software development. Systems engineer, marketing technical support. MIS manager.

5. **Special Opportunities in Computer Related Fields** 68
   Documentation: technical writers. Education. Medicine. Information science. Operations research. Industrial engineering.

6. **Education and Training** 77
   Preparing for the future. Learning on your own. High school. Two-year junior and community colleges. Four-year colleges and universities. Graduate study. Certification. Company-sponsored education and training. Keeping up with new developments.

7. **Finding a Job** 97
   Researching employers. On-campus recruitment. Letter-writing campaigns. Responding to ads. Using professional recruiters. Technical job fairs. On-line resources. Job application letters. Resumes. Preparing for a job interview. Some practical suggestions. Evaluating employment offers. Intangible job satisfactions.

8. **Employment Outlook: Shaping Your Career** 121
   Geographical distribution. Demand. Trends that may affect demand. Salary statistics. Career profiles. Some examples of typical career paths. Technology and market trends.

9. **Professional Organizations** 138
   User groups. Industry associations.

ABOUT THE AUTHOR

Julie Burns is an independent consultant providing market research and analysis to hardware and software vendors, including Apple, Borland, Component Integration Labs (CI Labs), Taligent, and others. Her clients benefit from her 15 years of industry experience in developing and marketing software products.

Prior to launching her consulting practice, Julie served as vice president of marketing for PeerLogic, Inc., a communications middleware vendor. In this role, she established the overall marketing direction for the company, including product positioning, marketing strategy, and channel development.

From 1986 to 1991, Julie held a wide range of positions in product, developer, technical, and channel marketing at Lotus Development Corporation. She was instrumental in launching such breakthrough products as Lotus Agenda, the first PIM, and Lotus Express, a pioneering PC-based electronic mail application. As marketing manager for networked products, Julie developed a keen understanding of today's networked computing environment. She also spearheaded development of a reseller program for Lotus Notes and other networked products.

Before joining Lotus, Julie worked on office automation and data communications products for Data General and as an independent consultant. She was a tenured member of the graduate faculty at Texas A&M University and also taught business communications at California State University, Long Beach. She has been a featured speaker at industry conferences and seminars.

Julie holds a B.A. from the University of California, Santa Cruz, and an M.A. and Ph.D. from the State University of New York at Buffalo.

FOREWORD

The opportunities are endless for a person who considers a career in the exciting world of computers. Challenging and rewarding positions are available in every area of business and in every corner of the world.

The 21st century will open doors for students in some industries that are relatively new to computerized techniques. Other doors will continue to open in established computerized businesses that need knowledgeable practitioners of the newest technologies. Imagine working on a cruise ship in the Caribbean or being part of a research team at IBM. These opportunities and others just as varied are available to computer science graduates.

The knowledge you have gained in high school is a substantial base for additional higher level education in computer science and business data processing. By building on your knowledge, you can open many doors in the growing and changing information processing industry.

Your career choice deserves all of the advantages it can use. In this fast paced, competitive business, any assistance you can give your résumé will help move you along your career path. For this reason, the Institute for Certification of Computer Professionals (ICCP) has developed a certification program just for people like you. The Associate Computer Professional (ACP) examination gives you a way to display your educational accomplishments on your résumé. The ACP was created to help entry-level personnel and beginning professionals boost their careers.

Joining a professional society is another way to assist you in defining your career goals and educational development. Professional societies with student chapters, such as the Association of Computing Management Association (DPMA), allow students to interact with professionals who have been successful in this ever-changing field. By joining a student chapter of a society, you can gain valuable knowledge from seasoned pros, you can learn about the day-to-day operations in the industry, and you can pinpoint the specialized area of the industry in which you would like to practice.

Choosing a career can be confusing and a little bit scary. Julie Kling Burns explores the challenging and interesting field of computer science and business data processing. Take advantage of all the information in this book, and then, if you decide to pursue a career in the field, join a student chapter in a professional society.

Your career will probably last at least thirty years. Research the career you want to become part of, question professionals, and be curious. Once you are sure, you will be able to offer only your best to one of the most exciting careers available today!

> George R. Eggert, CSP
> Executive Director
> Institute for Certification of Computer Professionals

INTRODUCTION

The purpose of this book is to help you explore some of the many exciting career opportunities available in computer software. We will look at what it's like to work inside the computer industry itself, where you may be designing, developing, or marketing the software that drives much of today's world. We will also see how you can use your software skills in other industries as an information systems professional.

Since you are reading this book, you have probably already had some experience with computers and computer software at school, at work, or at home. You or your family may have a computer at home—in 1995, over one in three households in the United States had one or more personal computers. Maybe you have already experimented with programming using applications like Microsoft Visual Basic or Apple's Hypercard. Or perhaps you are simply attracted to the field of computing because you have heard it offers many interesting and well-paying jobs.

In this book you will read about the kinds of work done by software professionals to bring new kinds of products to market that allow people to take advantage of rapid advances in technology. You will see how information systems professionals combine their education in software and business analysis to develop the applications that keep businesses up and running. And you will learn how your technical skills can lead to opportunities in sales and marketing. Finally, we will explore related opportunities in technical documentation, quality assurance, customer support, education, and even entertainment. (If you play Doom or any other game, you already know that software entertains.) Today, software professionals may even work in publishing, television, and the movie industry.

This book covers professional-level positions in the computer field: in other words, those career opportunities that usually—though not always—require a degree from a recognized four-year college or university. There are many opportunities for employment in computer-related positions that do not require a college education. Indeed, in today's society most jobs require that an employee be computer literate. There is a continuous demand for technicians, support staff, and computer operations personnel. These positions require limited or specialized vocational training only. Some require no previous training, as any instruction needed will be provided on the job by the employer. These positions can lead to wider opportunities. However, this book is designed to help you enter the software profession by way of your directly related education and experience.

We will also look at the personal characteristics and educational background you will need if you choose to become a computer professional. You will find advice on selecting a college or university program that will best prepare you for a career in computing. We will see how to go about finding your first job, and will describe the employment outlook and directions for future growth of the software industry.

Reading this book should help you to decide if a career in software development or information systems is for you. It will give you the information you will need if you decide to enter this exciting and rapidly expanding industry.

Some Definitions

As in any field, computer science has its own highly specialized vocabulary. Before we begin, let's review a few basic terms. In discussing computers, we talk about *hardware,* the physical equipment of a system, and *software,* the sets of instructions (or *programs*) that control the system and tell it how to solve specific problems. Programs are of two types: *applications programs* and *systems programs.* Applications programs are those sets of instructions written to perform a certain task or compute the answer to a particular problem. Microsoft Word and

Microsoft Excel are two examples of commonly used applications programs, as are the custom applications that your bank uses to process and keep track of your deposits and withdrawals. Systems programs direct, maintain, or otherwise assist the computer to operate and to execute applications programs. *Operating systems* such as Windows, OS/2, or UNIX are examples of systems programs. These programs oversee and direct all the operations of the machine.

Most application programs are written in *high-level languages* such as COBOL, Pascal, or C++. High-level languages resemble natural languages like English. (In fact, most high-level programming languages are English-based, and English is the dominant language of the worldwide computer community.) High-level languages are designed to make it easier for people to communicate with the machines. Some programming languages, such as SmallTalk or C++, are known as *object-oriented* languages. Other languages, such as LISP, are associated with specific areas of computer science. LISP is a program designed for building applications based on artificial intelligence. BASIC is a simple high-level language; Visual Basic is a development environment that makes it easier to program by providing developers with a visual "point and click" method to assemble applications. Indeed, use of Visual Basic and other high level development tools has made it easier for many companies to develop custom applications more quickly and with fewer bugs.

A computer, however, only understands *machine language.* This means that certain special kinds of systems programs, called *compilers,* must convert high-level languages into machine language—a code that will finally be reduced to a series of electronic signals.

The first step in solving any problem with a computer is to analyze it and develop a logical method for finding the solution. This method is called an *algorithm.* Next, the algorithm will be coded: that is, the programmer will write a program using an appropriate programming language (or high-level tool) that gives the computer step-by-step instructions on how to calculate or solve the problem, together with the data needed for its solution. Using CASE (Computer Aided Software Engineering) tools, the programmer may actually let the computer help to design the program. Next, this program, which can consist of many individual modules, will be linked and compiled by the system into *object code* before it can be run, or *executed*. Programs rarely run successfully the first time they are executed, however. Usually, the programmer must go back and find any and all mistakes in the program. This painstaking process is called *debugging*.

In order to solve most real-world problems, a program will need to obtain additional information, whether that information is stored in computer *memory* or is received as input from the user. For instance, a program written to keep track of your bank balance needs to know information about each withdrawal, check, and deposit. Such information is known as *data*. Some of this information can be entered by the user while running the program. Other information will be retrieved from memory where it has been collected and stored in *files* at some time previous to program execution.

Large organized collections (or *libraries*) of information are called *databases*. Databases may store information on a company's credit card customers, on all aspects of patient care and billing in a hospital, or on practically any subject. For instance, law enforcement professionals find out the owner of a vehicle by matching the license plate number against records stored in a database. The information revolution, the vast accumulation of knowledge made possible by microelectronics and computing, has made the database an important means of organizing this flood of facts so that it can be easily accessed and used.

Networking involves linking computers to one another over wires to create a *local* or *wide-area network*. Networking and data communications are the foundation of today's information culture. When you use a modem to dial up an on-line service such as Compuserve or America Online (AOL) or the Internet, you are taking advantage of networking technology. The latest developments in computer technology involve *multimedia,* the delivery of pictures, video, and sound to a personal computer. Multimedia content can be distributed on a CD ROM ("compact disk read-only memory") or over the network.

You will encounter these and other technical terms throughout this book. Some readers are undoubtedly already familiar with a range of technical jargon. If you're not, don't worry. One aim of this book is to assist you to learn more about the software industry, its language, and its people.

CHAPTER 1

A LOOK AT COMPUTERS AND COMPUTER CAREERS

Computers have invaded nearly every area of modern life. In any career you choose, there is a good chance that you will be involved with computers and computer software.

The phenomenal growth in the number of computer systems reflects their growing importance in almost every aspect of life. In 1947, computer engineer Howard Aiken predicted that six computers would satisfy the computing needs of the entire United States. By 1955, 244 computer systems were in use, and by 1980 this number had increased to over 600,000. In 1984, businesses and individuals in the United States purchased over two million computers. By 1994, worldwide shipments of personal computers and workstations were over 47 million.

Personal computers are now found in almost 40 percent of American households. As the number of computer systems has increased, so has the number of people who work with computers.

Computers are now used in every industry, from agriculture to aerospace. Farmers use computers to time the planting and harvesting of their crops. Ranchers no longer drive their herds to auction; they can sell their livestock in an electronic marketplace made possible by computer networks. In manufacturing, robots are programmed to assemble automobiles, weapons, and the electronic components used in computers themselves. Inventories are maintained, goods stored, and items pulled for sale in computerized warehouses designed to operate without human workers. In your local supermarket, computers combined with optical scanners serve as point-of-sale devices that automate your checkout. Computers help send manned spacecraft safely into orbit and aid physicians in diagnosing their patients' illnesses.

Artists use computers to create stunning graphics, and Hollywood uses them to produce spectacular special effects. Inside every Nintendo or Sega game machine is a sophisticated computer. Every time you make a plane reservation, phone a friend, or check your bank account statements, you are relying on computers. Computer technology wakes us in the morning, helps us in the kitchen, and follows us when we get into our car to drive to work. Computers can even be programmed to write poetry and to compose music.

You can combine an interest in computers with almost any profession or career. In this book, we explore the career opportunities available to individuals who specialize in computer science itself, and who want to be at the heart of this challenging field.

A BRIEF HISTORY OF COMPUTERS

Modern computers can perform rapid numerical calculations, store and retrieve information of every sort, and make logical decisions that sometimes approach the sophistication of human reasoning. These advanced electronic devices are the result of a number of technological needs and innovations.

The word "computer" derives from the original purpose for which these machines were designed: to quickly compute the answer to complex quantitative problems. People's desire for a mechanism that can reduce the time and repetitiveness of numerical calculations can be traced back to the invention of the abacus over 5,000 years ago. Devices made of pebbles or other movable counters were used in antiquity by the Chinese, Egyptians, Greeks, and Romans.

The first real calculating machine in the modern sense was built by French philosopher and mathematician Blaise Pascal (1623–1662). Pascal designed a system of wheels and dials to help his father maintain business accounts. This first desktop calculator could add and subtract numbers of up to eight digits. Today, Pascal's contribution to computer science and design is remembered in the computer language that bears his name, Pascal.

In the 1670s, another philosopher-mathematician, the German Gottfried Wilhelm Leibniz (1646–1716), developed a design for a more complex machine. Leibniz's "stepped reckoner" could not only add and subtract like Pascal's device; it could also multiply, divide, and find square roots. An unreliable working version of this machine was built by 1796, and by 1820 commercial versions were being sold.

The first true digital computer was designed by an eccentric Englishman named Charles Babbage (1791–1871). Working with his companion and colleague, Ada Lovelace (1815–1852), for whom the programming language Ada is named, Babbage spent most of his life trying to build his "analytical engine." Although a practical model was never completed, Babbage's ideas have been fundamentally important to the theory and design of modern computers.

The next major development in the history of the computer occurred in the United States in the last decades of the nineteenth century. Rapid population growth, the result of an increasing tide of European immigration, made it impossible for United States census officials to deal with a flood of new statistics. It took officials eight years to finish counting the results of the 1880 census. In order to speed up tabulation of the 1890 census, a young army engineer and statistician, Hermann Hollerith (1860–1929), constructed an electromechanical device that processed information stored on punched cards. Hollerith's invention reduced by two-thirds the time required to tabulate the 1890 census.

In using punched cards to store information, Hollerith had borrowed an idea from textile technology. The Jacquard loom, invented by Frenchman Joseph Marie Jacquard (1752–1834), used holes punched in cards as patterns to automate the weaving of complicated textile designs. In turn, Hollerith used the position of these holes to represent information on an individual's age, sex, nationality, and other vital statistics. For many years, Hollerith's code and punched cards were used for computer input (and sometimes output). The code can represent all 26 letters of the alphabet, as well as the digits zero through nine, as an arrangement of holes and spaces. Although punched cards have since become obsolete, remnants of Hollerith's code are still used to tell the computer how to read input and format output. And today we know the company originally formed by Hollerith, the Computing Tabulating Recording Company, as IBM.

ENIAC: The First Electronic Computer

Hollerith's machine was part electrical and part mechanical. The first fully electronic calculating machine, ENIAC (the Electronic Numerical Integrator and Computer) was developed in the early 1940s by J. Presper Eckert and John W. Mauchly. ENIAC was designed to help scientists and military personnel calculate the complex equations required by ballistics, and was one of the technical and scientific products of the effort by the United States to win the Second World War. (The other major product of the war effort was the atomic bomb.) ENIAC was a bulky construction of vacuum tubes, wiring, and other components. Weighing 30 tons, it took up a 30-by-50-foot room at the University of Pennsylvania's Moore School of Electrical Engineering, where Eckert and Mauchly worked. When fully operational in 1946, ENIAC could perform nearly 5,000 additions or subtractions a second; it could solve in two hours problems in nuclear physics that would have taken 100 human engineers an entire year to complete.

ENIAC greatly accelerated the speed of solving complex mathematical problems. However, it could not be programmed in the sense we understand the word today. Rather, it had to be rewired by hand to solve new problems. Moreover, whenever one of its nearly 19,000 vacuum tubes failed—which was not infrequently—the system stopped functioning correctly.

The invention of the transistor occurred in 1948 at Bell Telephone Laboratories, greatly increasing the reliability and speed of subsequent computers. It also reduced the machine to a more manageable size. Transistors could be wired onto circuit boards to create permanent circuits to hold, send, or convert electrical impulses. These circuits made it possible to "hard-wire" basic operations into the computer system itself, and replaced the bulky and fickle vacuum tubes with smaller, more reliable components.

John von Neumann

The idea of storing computer instructions in the machine itself was advanced by mathematician John von Neumann (1903–1957) in 1947. His "stored program" notion revolutionized the speed and ease with which the computer could be used to solve problems. ENIAC required that computer instructions be entered into the machine by disconnecting and reconnecting by hand the many individual electrical connections. Von Neumann realized that these instructions could be coded as numbers and stored electronically in the same way as the numbers used in the actual calculations. This allowed sequences of instructions—programs—to be loaded electronically into the machine, eliminating the time-consuming task of hand setting the instruction sequence for each task.

Von Neumann was also responsible for defining the basic structure (or *architecture*) of the modern electronic digital computer: its division into input/output, arithmetic-logic and control units, and memory.

Input and output devices enable us to communicate with the computer, giving it raw data and the instructions (or program) to process that information. Output devices supply us with the results of the computer's calculations or data processing operations. As we have seen, in the early days of computing, punched cards were used for both input and output. Today, a variety of different input and output devices are available. Most familiar is the alphanumeric keyboard and television screen, or cathode ray tube (CRT). Combined, these devices are called VDTs (for "video display terminal"). Other input/output (I/O) devices include optical character readers (OCRs), scanners, page readers, disks, magnetic tape, and—for output only—a wide variety of printers, some using laser technology to print an astonishing 120 pages per minute. Recent developments in computer I/O include voice processing, compact disks, and digital audio tape (DAT). Special devices have also been developed that help handicapped individuals interact with computers. Devices like the mouse, which allows computer users to point, select, and move words and images of the computer screen, are becoming standard. More futuristic ways of interacting with computers are no longer only in the realm of fantasy and science fiction. In combination with advanced software and graphics, specialized hardware makes it possible for a computer user to interact with a wholly imaginary world as if it were real.

The *central processing unit* (CPU) is the heart of the computer system. It consists essentially of two parts: an *arithmetic-logic unit* (ALU) and a *control unit*. The control unit monitors all system operations, reading instructions and passing instructions and data to the ALU, where actual computations take place. But the CPU has a limited amount of space or *memory* in which to store data and instructions. Thus additional memory is located outside of the computer core. With the help of the operating system and the executing program, information is fetched from memory and brought into the CPU. The results of each computation are likewise stored in memory.

Most computers currently in use today, from small home computers to large-scale mainframes, conform to the basic structure described by von Neumann. New machines, however, are being developed along very different patterns of organization. Using parallel processing or neural networks, these machines vastly extend the limited computational power of the classic von Neumann machine.

Integrated Circuits

In the 1950s, advances in memory technology increased the amount of information that could be stored and processed by the computer. Magnetic core, tape, and later (in the 1960s) disk storage dramatically expanded the power of the machines. Improved reliability and increased memory capacity made computers attractive to businesses with large data processing needs. Computers began to appear in business and industry as scientists discovered that they could program the machines to select and process alphabetical information as well as operate on numbers.

Computers probably would have remained relatively specialized machines, expensive and with limited applications, without the invention of the semiconductor integrated circuit. Before integrated circuitry, the individual components of the circuitry of a computer or any other electronic device—transistors, capacitors, and so on—were connected by copper wiring. The speed of a computer is a factor of the distance electrical signals must travel. To increase computational speed, you have to reduce this distance. Hand-wired circuits and individual components could only be scaled down so far.

By the 1950s, a process called photolithography had been developed that made it possible to "print" the wiring connecting circuit components in much the same way that a photograph is produced from a negative. This made it possible to reduce the distance between components, but, though vastly smaller than the vacuum tubes they had replaced, the components themselves remained relatively large. Researchers came up with a novel idea: If the wiring could be photolithographically printed, would it not be possible to "print" the components themselves using the same process to etch them out of a semiconductive material like silicon? In this way, the wiring and the components of a circuit could be simultaneously produced out of the same layered wafer of semiconductive and other materials. The complexity of the circuit to be produced would determine the number of "printings" necessary. Thus was born the integrated circuit, the field of microelectronics, and the information revolution of which we are all a part.

Today, the computational power of ENIAC and more can be contained on a single microchip. "Supercomputers," extremely powerful number-crunchers like those manufactured by companies such as Cray, can perform over millions of operations per second. Intel doubles the power of its chips, which have fueled the desktop PC revolution, every 18 months. New developments in computer science theory and applications occur daily as the physical and logical limits of present systems are surpassed. The field of computer science offers an unparalleled and exciting opportunity for highly motivated individuals with the right interests, abilities, and education.

HARDWARE AND SOFTWARE PROFESSIONALS

In general, we can divide computer professionals into two main classes: hardware engineers and software specialists. In this book, we are mainly interested in software.

Hardware specialists design and develop new systems, from chips to complete systems. People who specialize in hardware usually have a background in electrical engineering and hardware design. They work in the manufacturing sector of the computer industry for companies such as Intel, Texas Instruments, Apple, IBM, 3Com, or Cisco. The products they produce range from chips and circuits to complete computers and specialized hardware like network adaptors, routers, or embedded systems (specialized computers used in everything from automobiles to airplanes).

Software specialists program the software that runs on hardware. Software developers fall into two broad categories: those who work on *systems software* and those who write *application software.* Systems software includes "firmware" (the low-level programming instructions built into hardware to tell it how to operate), operating system software (like Windows NT, MacOS, or Unix), communications, and other special kinds of programs. Systems software also includes software tools (used to build applications) and utilities (housekeeping programs). Application software refers to everything else. Games, electronic mail, word processors, the software that runs banks or lets you make airline reservations—all these and more are software applications.

WHERE DO COMPUTER PROFESSIONALS WORK?

Industry Sectors

Computer personnel, including programmers, systems analysts, operators, and technicians, work in nearly every sector of the U.S. economy. Four major industries, however, account for the bulk of computer-related employment:

Services. Colleges and universities, accounting and other business services, hospitals and health care facilities—all employ computer specialists, primarily in data processing. Computer consulting services, which provide programming, systems design, and product support to other businesses, employ technical and business computer experts.

Manufacturing. Computer hardware, software, and peripheral equipment vendors naturally employ many computer specialists. And as the manufacturing of every kind of product becomes increasingly automated, many computer professionals will be needed to design and program the production machinery and software and maintain the automatic manufacturing systems.

Finance, Insurance, and Real Estate. Banks and insurance companies process enormous quantities of data. These industries are principal employers of data processing and information management specialists. Indeed, the computerization of the financial services industry has created many new investment instruments—as well as many new jobs.

Wholesale and Retail Trade. Computers are used to control inventory, record sales, and control the daily operations in wholesale and retail business, from the neighborhood supermarket and local department store to industrial suppliers and distributors. Although most people working with computers in the trade are not experts, there are exceptions. First, computer specialists are needed to write programs and develop systems for this industry. Second, many computer specialists are needed to sell and service computer equipment and software.

Computer personnel are also employed in transportation; communications; public utilities; federal, state, and local government; and the military. Computers and computer professionals are even found in mining, fishing, and agriculture. Computers help tuna fishers off the Pacific coast to find schools of fish, allow ranchers to improve cattle-breeding programs, and help farmers predict insect activity that threatens their crops.

It is important to note that the growth of computer use in any industry has so far not been tied to the expansion of that industry. Rather, increased opportunities for computer-related employment are the product of expanded applications of computers to that field.

The computer field is dynamic and rapidly changing. This makes it hard to draw clear distinctions, especially as many people with different job titles may perform similar duties. For instance, a field engineer at one company may be called a customer engineer at another. On the other hand, the same job title may be used to describe different kinds of functions. A programmer/analyst in a bank may have very different responsibilities than someone with the same title working for an engineering and construction firm.

TYPES OF EMPLOYERS

In the jargon of computer professionals, there are two types of employer: vendors and end-users (or just "users"). If you work inside the computer hardware and software industry, you will work for a vendor, a company that produces computer products. If you work in any other industry, you will be working for a user organization.

Vendors

Vendors include manufacturers of large and small general purpose computers and peripheral devices. Many of these vendors have become household names: IBM, Apple, Hewlett Packard. Other vendors specialize in special purpose computer systems or equipment. Cray, Stratus, and Tandem, for example, manufacture computers designed with unique architectures devised for special kinds of processing. Toshiba has focused on making high-performance laptop computers; US Robotics currently sets the standard for modem manufacturing. Cisco Systems and BayNet provide the infrastructure for internetworks. Other companies limit their business to the manufacture of components such as printers, scanners, input devices, CD-ROM drives, or backup systems. Motorola, Intel, and AMD, among others, manufacture the microprocessors that form the basis of personal computers and workstations.

Software companies develop, sell, and support system software and application programs. Microsoft, for instance, provides the operating and windowing systems for PC compatible computers. Lotus Development Corporation, which has been purchased by IBM, develops individual and group business productivity software for many different computers. Broderbund and Electronic Arts are major providers of game and educational software, while Borland International now specializes in programming tools and languages. Novell and Artisoft focus on networking software, while Oracle, Informix, and Sybase concentrate on database management systems.

Computer service companies, distributors, resellers and system integrators all work to match vendor offerings with customer needs. They may also provide consulting services, maintenance, and support to end-user organizations.

Within a vendor organization, there are a number of specialized functions:

- *Development.* Development designs and implements the product.
- *Quality assurance.* Quality assurance staff (QA) tests the product to make sure it functions as designed.
- *Customer support.* Customer support personnel assist customers who are having problems using the product.
- *Sales and marketing.* The sales team helps customers understand how the product will help them in their own business. Marketing personnel help development staff understand customer requirements and determine product pricing, distribution, and promotion.
- *Documentation.* Documentation specialists write manuals and develop on-line systems to tell the customer how to use the product.
- *Training.* The training organization develops curricula and teaches courses that help people learn how to use the product.

Many large computer companies are organized by function. Smaller companies, or those companies with a strong product team approach, will group employees on the basis of a particular product.

Both functional and product organizations have benefits. For instance, you may have more opportunity for technical growth when you work with a large group of developers or QA engineers, many of whom will have had several years of experience. On the other hand, working as part of a product team you will learn about the many different aspects of getting a product to market. This diverse experience will be helpful to you if you plan to go into management or want to move into other areas, such as sales or marketing.

Working for End User Organizations

If you work for a company outside of the computer industry, you will work as part of the information systems team to provide computer support to the business operations of the organization. MIS, "management information systems," IS, "information systems," and IT, "information technology" are all terms used to describe this mission. In large corporations like CitiBank or Bank of America, the number of IS professionals may be in the hundreds or even thousands. In small companies, a single person may be responsible for everything to do with the computers and software used to run the business.

Some companies have a single business unit or division devoted to corporate MIS. At other companies, those responsible for hardware and software may work for individual business units like sales, manufacturing, or engineering.

Corporate IS job functions include:

MIS and data processing staff. In companies with large mainframe and client-server systems, the MIS staff determines processing needs, purchases equipment and software, installs and maintains the systems, and writes custom applications to handle the day-to-day flow of information. The MIS organization processes payroll, accounts payable, accounts receivable, and other financial tasks. They also manage the databases of corporate information stored on these large computers.

The Information Center. In some large companies with many personal computers, the "info center" staff serve the PC user community. Info center personnel evaluate and recommend new products, develop custom applications, install and configure the products, and help people to use the software. Increasingly, corporate MIS handles much of the work once done by the info center.

Network administration. Companies purchase computers of many types, and many employees now view computer resources as vital to doing their job. By networking computers together, people can share information and equipment such as printers. In this networked environment, network administrators are the ones who keep everything running.

Data communications and telecommunications. Data and telecommunications staff (which may include network administrators) are responsible for the overall selection, maintenance, and support of the wiring, hardware, software, and services that provide voice and data communications within a large organization.

Small and large businesses alike hire information specialists. Banks, insurance companies, and other financial institutions are major employers of information and data processing specialists. Applications experts can find opportunities in any corporation or business where there is a need for financial reports, analysis of business trends, or record keeping.

IS A JOB IN COMPUTER SOFTWARE FOR YOU?

Certainly, the computer field presents many rewarding career opportunities. However, is it the right field for you? You should go through three steps in making a career decision:
- Identify your skills, aptitudes, and interests
- Identify a career or profession where you can use your skills
- Identify the education and practical job experience you will need to attain your career goals

In order to identify your aptitudes and interests, begin by asking yourself some simple questions. What classes have you done well in, and enjoyed, in school? What are your hobbies and extracurricular activities? How do you like to spend your free time? Make a list of what you feel to be your major accomplishments. Which have been most important to you? Which have given you greatest satisfaction?

Your school counseling or placement office may be able to help you assess your abilities. Standardized vocational guidance testing is often available. Your school may even have a computerized vocational guidance program, like the Educational Testing Service's SIGI.

Many books available in your library or local bookstore are good sources of vocational advice. One book that you may find very helpful in identifying your particular talents is Richard Bolles's widely read *What Color Is Your Parachute?* (Ten Speed Press). Bolles's book is updated annually and includes a good deal of practical career advice.

What kind of person will flourish in computer science? How do you know if computing is for you? For some people, an aptitude for computer science may be as obvious as a gift for music or mathematics. If you are a computer whiz or natural programmer, someone with endless curiosity about and enthusiasm for the machines and what they do, you have probably already decided to go into computer science and are reading this book to find out how to do it.

But what if you are not certain that computer science is for you? If you have not yet decided on a career, you must ask yourself to what extent you have the attributes of a successful computer expert. Computers are logical and they reward logical thought. If you are logical, systematic, and patient, and if you enjoy solving problems or puzzles, computing may be for you. Mathematical abilities can be helpful in systems programming, data communications, scientific and engineering applications, and in research and development. Math is less important in business and many other applications. Written and oral communication skills are very important. Positions in marketing, sales, customer support, or management require excellent interpersonal skills as well.

More difficult to describe, but often a key trait found among persons who are successful in the field of computing, is a kind of creative delight in making things work. The best programmers often combine a logical, analytical approach with intuitive insight to solve problems or design products that meet customer needs. Many of the best programmers are also active in another field—for instance, history, music, or the visual arts. You will find that people who do well in computers usually have a high level of intellectual curiosity about the world in general and how it works.

The following list summarizes the traits of the type of individual who is likely to find computer science a rewarding and satisfying profession:

- A capacity for logical thought
- Analytical skills: enjoys solving problems or puzzles
- Mental ingenuity or cunning: an ability to see more than one way to do something
- Painstaking attention to detail
- Persistence: able to stick with a problem until it is completely worked out
- Good communication skills
- Creativity and intellectual curiosity

In addition to these traits, you will need well-developed study habits if you wish to prepare for a career in computer science. You must also enjoy and be committed to learning. A degree in computer science is only the first step in your education as a professional in this field. The pace of development and the variety of individual applications mean that the computer professional's education never stops. On-the-job training and continuing education are essential.

If you possess these attributes, together with a mechanical aptitude, and like the idea of working with computer hardware—the electrical "nuts and bolts" of the machines—you may want to consider the related field of electrical engineering. If you are intrigued by the connection between machine and program, are attracted to the problem-solving challenge of programming, want to learn about the theoretical problems behind a computer system and its organization, or are interested in the ways that computers can be used in other fields, computer software may be for you. And if you want to combine an interest in computers with the opportunity to work with other people, you might want to consider a career in marketing, sales, education, or customer support.

The range of opportunities for individuals with computer science expertise is vast. Perhaps you will contribute to the design and programming of ever-faster, more powerful machines. As a member of a project team, you might program and track the flight of the space shuttle or develop special systems that enable blind persons to "see" and the deaf to "hear" again. You might study the way we think and speak, in order to create an intelligent computer that imitates human thought or understands human speech. Maybe you will gain satisfaction from teaching others how to use and enjoy computers, or work in business applications in banking, insurance, or any of a number of different fields. You could manage the information system of a hospital or university, or help businesses to select, install, and maintain a computer system that meets their specific needs. These and many other possibilities are yours if you choose to pursue a career in computer science.

CHAPTER 2

WORKING INSIDE THE COMPUTER INDUSTRY

In this chapter, we will look at the kinds of opportunities available if you work for a manufacturer of computer hardware, software, or services. This will include:

- Hardware product development. Although the emphasis of this book is on job opportunities in software, we will look briefly at hardware product development, because many systems-level programming jobs are with manufacturers of computer chips, peripherals, or systems.
- Software product development. Many of the exciting software jobs are for software vendors. We will look at what it is like to work as part of a development team.
- Research and development. Large companies such as IBM, AT&T, or Hewlett Packard invest in substantial research that may or may not lead directly to new revenue-producing products.
- Working for a start-up. Companies such as Apple and Microsoft were born out of the hard work of a small group of dedicated developers. We will look at the pros and cons of working for a start-up.

In addition, we will look at a few of the many opportunities for people with technical skills to move into sales and marketing.

Because the computer industry changes so rapidly, it is impossible to cover every opportunity that exists. Rather, we will look at some typical career opportunities to give you an idea of what it would be like to work as part of the computer industry.

HARDWARE PRODUCT DEVELOPMENT

The word *hardware* is used to designate the physical units or equipment that make up a computer system: the computer itself and its network of microchips and circuitry, as well as peripheral equipment such as terminals, printers, and drives.

Computer scientists and software engineers work with electrical engineers and other equipment design specialists to design, develop, and test computer hardware and peripheral equipment. Design of hardware can range from the creation of a single computer chip, such as Intel's Pentium microprocessor, to an entire computer system or product. But since computers are made up of an array of microprocessors and memory chips, much of the work in hardware takes place at the chip level.

Peripheral equipment may be developed in conjunction with the computer design as part of a total system. Or it may be developed independently. Some companies, such as Radius or Logitech, specialize in producing peripherals—in this case, monitors and pointing devices—that can be used with computers built by different manufacturers.

A hardware product begins as an idea or concept. A team of engineers and computer science experts get together and ask: "What would we (or our customers) like to see in a product? What problem can we solve?" For instance, Hewlett Packard constantly designs new and improved printers to meet customers' demands for faster, high-definition, and even color printing. Once the general idea is sketched out, a set of engineering specifications is developed. These specifications express in complete detail the performance, design, and material characteristics of the product. The next step is to build a prototype, or working model, which is tested, debugged, and perfected before full-scale manufacturing begins.

What does this process involve at the chip level? Once the performance specifications have been formalized, electrical and computer engineers develop logic and circuit designs. These patterns lay out the path electrons will travel as signals are pulsed through the chip. These circuit designs are photographically enlarged and studied. Any flaws are corrected. Then, each circuit design is reduced to a "photomask" or negative, which is used to etch or imprint the circuit onto a silicon wafer. The manufacture of silicon chips is complex and must take place under extremely sterile conditions. One bit of dust can make a chip unusable. The technology that has been developed to manufacture computer chips is extraordinarily sophisticated; many manufacturing procedures are closely guarded secrets.

Before chips go into full production, the prototype is rigorously tested to locate any potential error. Quality assurance engineers write special test programs to evaluate prototype performance. At every stage in the development of computer hardware and at any level, testing and evaluation are crucial. To detect the slightest potential for error, test specialists try to subject the prototype to all possible input situations. Many flaws are only found through endless trial-and-error testing.

Hardware engineers are involved in logic design and testing, microprogramming, systems design—linking individual chips into a fully-operational system—and systems evaluation. All careers in hardware require a solid background in electrical engineering. You should plan your undergraduate program to include hardware design, electrical engineering, and physics courses if you want to work in this area. You should consider colleges and college curricula that specialize in computer engineering. More detailed information on careers in engineering can be found in VGM's book, *Opportunities in Engineering Careers.*

SOFTWARE PRODUCT DEVELOPMENT

In the early days of computers and computing, the emphasis was placed on improving hardware design to increase the speed and reliability of operations. When integrated circuitry was introduced in the 1960s, however, machines became virtually fail-safe and much less costly. From this point on many, if not most, computer errors could really be attributed to human error: that is, to errors in software programming. Moreover, the extension of computer applications into many areas of life depends on writing new sets of instructions to tell the machine how to perform new tasks. Recent breakthroughs in materials science and superconductivity, as well as continuing advances in chip technology, suggest that hardware development will continue to offer many rewarding career opportunities. Nonetheless, some industry experts feel the astonishingly rapid advances in hardware technology may be over. They believe that, while hardware development will continue, the most exciting and creative advances in the future will take place in software.

Software Engineering

Software has become increasingly complex as customers have asked for more and more functionality. When Lotus 1-2-3, the first widely used spreadsheet program, was introduced in October 1982, it could be run from a single floppy disk. The 1995 version of 1-2-3 required four megabytes of memory to run. It took 250 "developer years" (equal to one programmer working for an entire year) to develop the *sixth* version of a popular wordprocessor—and another 45 developer years to fix the bugs! Recent trends in personal computer software look to the use of object-oriented programming and plug-and-play software modules or components promise to reduce the effort required to develop commercial software. Nevertheless, development of feature-rich software will still require a disciplined approach. This disciplined approach to the design and development of software is called *software engineering*.

Central to software engineering is the idea of the *software life cycle*, which breaks the design, development, and maintenance of large programs into a series of interrelated steps:

- Identification of what the software must be able to do. This is sometimes called "requirements engineering" and produces the "functional specification" or "spec."
- Description of how the software will accomplish the tasks it must do. In this stage, software engineers develop a design specification that outlines major sections of the program.
- Implementation. At this point, members of a programming team work individually to code and debug segments of the program. Structured programming techniques, first proposed by E. Dijkstra in 1968, enable the software engineer to see the program as a series of separate units. More recently, the use of object-oriented design methodologies has proved effective in modularizing the development of code. Each unit can be assigned to a different programmer, then assembled into the overall software system.

- Testing and validation. In this phase, the program is tested using sample input to make sure that it performs correctly and to locate any possible sources of errors.
- Operations and maintenance. The task of the software engineer is not over when the system is installed and running. Maintaining and updating the program will continue as long as it is being used. It is estimated that between 40 to 60 percent of the money spent on software goes to its maintenance.

The development of a new computer product involves much more than its design. It includes following a product from its first idea through its manufacturing and marketing phases. It may include changing or upgrading the product as it is improved or as customers need additional features. Most computer software, for instance, is periodically updated by its vendor. This means all users must be notified and changes in individual installations made. In fact, from a computer vendor's point of view, development does not end until a product is withdrawn from the market.

Software engineering describes both a method and a job classification. Many senior programmers working as part of a development team hold the title of software engineer. Software engineers usually have a degree in computer science (although this is not a requirement) and several years of experience designing software. Senior software engineers are often called architects, reflecting their role in determining how software will be built.

The Product Team

Programmers almost always work as part of a project or product team. This team usually includes a project leader or development manager, who may be a senior software engineer. The development manager often reports to a product manager, who is responsible for all aspects of the product, or to a department head. The project leader is responsible for overall program design and assigns programming tasks to other team members. This individual is assisted by an experienced senior programmer or architect who supervises other programmers, checks their work, and confers with the project leader when problems arise.

Programmers translate the design specifications into computer code. They work on small segments of the program at a time, writing code, using sample data to test and debug each piece of code, and making changes to eliminate errors in their segments.

The most important goal of any project team is to get the product ready for customers and out the door. To ship a product requires the coordination of many people and many functions. Programmers must work in cooperation with other team members who help bring the product to market. Any product team will include quality assurance engineers, documentation staff, and marketing, in addition to development. It may also include a development or product manager. In some organizations, the product manager has profit-and-loss responsibility; his or her compensation may be directly tied to how well the product fares in the marketplace.

The quality assurance (QA) staff tests programmers' code and returns it to the programmer who wrote it for "bug fixes." Technical writers and editors work with programmers and marketing to produce printed and electronic documentation. The product marketing personnel work with customers to make sure the product meets their needs. They also work with advertising and public relations groups. An administrative assistant may handle the allocation of money, office space, personnel, and equipment, as well as daily office routines. This frees the product manager to attend to technical design as well as handle business issues. A program librarian or manager may be assigned to keep track of the status of program modules and progress against the team schedule. A program manager may also work with manufacturing, distribution, creative services, and other groups to make sure everything related to the product is completed on time.

The size and composition of a product team will vary with the scope and complexity of the project and may depend on whether a company is organized according to function or by product team. Regardless of the makeup of the team, it is important for programmers to realize that many people with expertise in many different areas must work together to create a software product.

Most recent computer science graduates will begin as junior programmers or coders, working on a project that may already be well-advanced. Beginning programmers work to modify sections of code written by more senior programmers, then progress to write sections of original code and to develop testing procedures for debugging.

Working as part of a product team can be an intense experience. Most projects are completed under extreme time pressure: it may not matter how elegantly you write a program. The point is to get the system up and running. Most programming teams work against deadlines set by other divisions of their organization. It is not uncommon for team members to work after hours and even on weekends when a deadline is approaching. In some environments, team members have been known to move toaster ovens and sleeping bags into their offices and to work days at a stretch. Meals may be brought in; 2 A.M. meetings are not unheard of.

To work successfully under such stressful conditions requires more than mere technical competence. Nerves are frayed, tempers are short, people are anxious and often very tired. Patience, self-control, sensitivity to the feelings and concerns of other team members, and simple stamina are valuable traits in such circumstances. These traits may have little to do with a programmer's technical ability.

Systems Software Programming

Systems programmers specify, design, and develop operating systems, compilers, assemblers, debuggers, utility and database management programs, and other kinds of software that direct entire computer systems and enable higher-level applications to be processed. Systems programmers also install, debug, and maintain systems software once it is in place.

Systems programmers may work for computer hardware, software, and peripheral manufacturers; computer service companies; management consulting firms; or (more rarely) in end-user organizations.

Working for computer manufacturers, systems programmers work with design teams to develop new computer systems or products and to upgrade existing systems. They often assist in the installation of a system purchased by a customer and may help train the customer's employees in the use of their new system.

Working in an end-user environment, systems software programmers support their organization's computer operations and applications programming. They help applications people evaluate their computing needs, and ensure that all systems function efficiently and accurately. They modify vendor software packages to meet the needs of their own company and sometimes are responsible for the security of the computer system.

The proliferation of personal computers and networking in a variety of industries and applications has created a need for systems programmers who can work with distributed systems. The systems programming requirements for a network of small computers differ from those of a centralized mainframe computer. At present, systems programmers with expertise in data communications, networking, database concepts, and client-server applications are very much in demand.

Systems programmers work mainly with assembly languages or C rather than with the high-level languages used in applications programming. Assembly languages are closer to the code of ones and zeros that the machine understands than they are to the more "natural" high-level languages. Assembly language programming is rigorous and extremely detailed. It demands of the programmer not only acute analytical skills, but patience, persistence, and precision. It also takes a special sort of intuitive problem-solving creativity that most systems programmers talk about but find difficult to define.

People who go into systems programming tend to be more interested in problems in pure computer science than in the kinds of problems in science, business, or entertainment that are of principal concern to applications programmers. Systems programmers may also need some interest in hardware.

Systems software programmers usually begin, like most programmers, as coders working on programs designed and developed by systems groups. They may then advance from senior systems programmer level to systems project leader, heading a team of systems specialists in the design and implementation of systems software. Advancement in end-user organizations can lead to operations management and technical support positions.

Engineering and/or Scientific Applications Programming

Applications programmers working in a scientific or engineering environment design, code, test, and debug programs to solve specific technical or theoretical problems. These problems almost always involve complex mathematical calculations. Programmers in this field also help to develop the hardware, software, and input/output specifications for computer systems used in scientific and engineering applications.

Computer vendors employ engineering applications programmers to assist in product development and support. Some companies sponsor high-level research related to physics and mathematics. Much programming on these projects will be done by the researchers themselves, assisted by applications programmers. Engineering and scientific applications programmers may also work in many different industries, including aerospace and avionics, defense-related research and development, telecommunications, manufacturing, medical research and treatment, the oil and gas industry, and in all fields of engineering.

Applications programmers in a scientific or engineering environment aid in the work that pushes science and technology beyond the limits of the present. They may solve problems in "real-time" control systems, where the computer must sense external conditions and respond immediately; for example, in the computer system that guides a missile in its flight from launch to target or controls the temperature of a manufacturing process. They may write the software that links a network of computers and monitoring devices into a single, fully automated production line, or the software that processes the images beamed back to earth from space. Applications programmers use special simulation or graphics languages to develop models to improve the flow of raw materials through a manufacturing plant or of air around the surface of an accelerating automobile. They write programs to plot the orbit of a satellite, probe the depths of the earth in search of oil, track the path of an approaching hurricane, or predict the long-range effects of a disaster on the surrounding population and environment.

The solution of many complex scientific problems requires the computational power of a supercomputer. At the same time, though, powerful, high-resolution workstations such as those produced by Sun, Silicon

Graphics, and other vendors (including IBM and Digital) have greatly expanded the market for scientific and engineering applications. These machines provide considerable processing power combined with high-quality graphics displays in a desktop computer.

A programmer specializing in scientific and engineering applications should have a knowledge of Unix and will use languages such as FORTRAN, still used for scientific programming, C, and assembly languages. Ada, a language commissioned by the U.S. Department of Defense (DOD) to replace FORTRAN, is also used for aerospace, energy, and military research funded by the DOD.

In addition to a knowledge of assembly and high-level programming languages, you should have excellent mathematical skills to work in this field. You also need good interpersonal skills and the ability to listen. Scientific and engineering applications programmers work in tightly knit, small teams and must often confer with scientists or engineers to determine what their problems are, what input they can supply, and what output they expect. Because this kind of programming requires a high level of mathematical and technical knowledge, many people working in the field today hold degrees in mathematics, physics, or other sciences, or in an engineering discipline other than computer science.

DEVELOPING SHRINK-WRAP AND COMMERCIAL SOFTWARE

The bulk of software companies in the computer industry design and market shrink-wrap or commercial software. "Shrink-wrap" refers to personal computer applications that are typically sold to individuals through retail stores, direct mail, or other channels; shrink-wrap is the clear plastic covering that protects the box containing the media—either diskettes or CD ROM—and a user's manual. Of course, not all shrink-wrap software is distributed through retailers. It can come bundled with personal computers or customers may download it from the Internet.

Because of the sheer number of PCs, producing and selling shrink-wrap software is a major business, with many opportunities for software developers. At one time, most shrink-wrap software was designed to improve business productivity, for example, spreadsheets, word processors, business graphics, and databases. The increased number of PCs sold to home users, especially those who now have multimedia capabilities, has led to an explosion of the varieties of shrink-wrap software. Games like Doom and Myst, personal finance like Quicken, and personal organizer products like SideKick are only a few of the more widely known shrink-wrap products.

Commercial software also includes products that are designed for large businesses and can be run on networked PCs, mid-range systems, or mainframes. Often, these products are developed for a specific "vertical" industry: for instance, healthcare, insurance, or real estate. Or they may perform a specific business function: payroll, accounting, inventory control. More exotic kinds of commercial software include digital video and special effect graphics, as well as applications developed for the Internet.

Some of the most exciting and challenging opportunities in software can be found in shrink-wrap and commercial product development. This means that competition for jobs with these companies can be intense. You will need first-rate technical skills, the ability to work as part of a team, and a willingness to give up personal time in the interests of getting the product out the door.

Development Manager

Development managers coordinate all aspects of a specific hardware or software development project. These individuals plan, direct, and supervise the efforts of the project team. They schedule the work and write the progress reports. They also serve as a link between the project team and other divisions and departments.

Development managers need the technical background and experience that will enable them to assist in product development. In addition, successful development managers have exceptional interpersonal skills. This job requires working closely with a limited number of technical people and non-technical support staff. It is up to the development manager to motivate employees, maintain group harmony and productivity, and build the team.

Promotion to development manager comes from senior programming and project leader positions. Development managers may have limited financial responsibility, but they are expected to remain in close contact with technical developments.

The development manager position can be a steppingstone to the higher echelons of management. In large vendor organizations, development management also provides a niche for the technically minded individual more interested in bits and bytes than in profit and loss.

Product Manager

The product manager has final responsibility for all aspects of a software or hardware product, including development and marketing. In small companies or companies with a strong product team approach, the product manager supervises the development manager, marketing manager, and the documentation and quality assurance personnel. He or she has profit-and-loss responsibility and must manage the development budget, including revenue projections.

In many companies, the product manager frequently has a background in marketing rather than technical management. His or her business sense must be supplemented by an understanding of the technical issues involved in the product and by experience of the development process. In some cases, however, especially in new companies or companies developing advanced products, a development manager can advance to a product manager position.

RESEARCH AND DEVELOPMENT (R&D)

Research is the study of the fundamental physical and theoretical problems in a field, without direct concern for practical applications. *Development* applies the findings of basic research to solve concrete problems or to design products that fulfill specific needs or perform particular tasks. Of course, the line between basic research and practical applications is never clear. In many vendor organizations, "R&D" is synonymous with product development. At the same time, however, advances in theoretical knowledge make it possible to develop new products. Furthermore, new innovations in technology may shed light on previously unexplained theoretical questions.

Most corporate research in computer science is closely tied to product development and manufacturing support. Much applied research takes place in vendor organizations, while the more theoretical research is typically done in university settings, often supported by funding from industry or government.

Large companies such as IBM and AT&T devote substantial amounts of their budget to applied research. For example, much of the fundamental research into superconductivity has been performed at IBM research centers. (Superconductivity refers to the ability of certain materials to conduct electricity. These materials may help engineers to design faster, more powerful computers.) AT&T has always sponsored fundamental research at its famous Bell Labs.

Positions in software research and development are available in nearly every area of computer science, including computational methods and numerical analysis (developing new algorithms and solving difficult problems in advanced mathematics); computer organization and architecture (devising ways to improve computer performance by changing the relation of a computer's parts and structure); systems design and systems science (studying computer operations and applications as a network of functions); telecommunications and network optimization; programming systems and languages (pushing the applications of computers in new directions through increased knowledge of programming techniques, linguistics, and natural languages); and information science (designing ways to make more information more readily available to users). Many positions in research and development require graduate study; some require a Ph.D. in computer science or a related discipline.

Current Directions in Research

The field of computer science changes rapidly. Today's topic of advanced research rapidly becomes tomorrow's product. As computer systems become more sophisticated, progress in one area of research often quickly leads to progress on another front. In the following paragraphs, we describe some of the ongoing research efforts in computer science.

COMPUTER ARCHITECTURE

Most computers are based on the structure (or "architecture") associated with John von Neumann; all process a sequential string of instructions and deal with only one instruction at a time. Improvements in computational speed result from increasingly compact, reliable circuitry. In order to make the quantuum leap in performance that today's most powerful machines require, this one-operation-at-a-time architecture must be surpassed. Researchers believe that parallel processing—linking a number of processors together, each of which simultaneously executes an instruction—will expand the computational limits of present machines. We know that the human brain is able to process many kinds of information at the same time: we can simultaneously listen to the radio, eat an apple, and drive a car through the rush hour traffic. We think and make decisions on the basis of multiple stimuli. Designing a computer that can compute more quickly or "think" in human terms will depend in part on developments in parallel processing. Already, a number of companies are building computers based on this alternative architecture.

VERY LARGE-SCALE INTEGRATED CIRCUITS

The microelectronics revolution that replaced slide rules with pocket calculators and placed the computer next to the television set in many American homes was made possible by integrated circuitry and the silicon chip. While most research efforts today focus on advanced software, this earlier software runs on microprocessors and memory chips. The research problems in VLSI include inventing new design techniques to improve the performance of these miniaturized circuits and the manufacturing techniques that enable over a million transistors to be crammed onto a single chip that can be economically mass produced. VLSI research covers work in basic physics, circuit design, materials and manufacturing, and developing improved ways to link chips together. Breakthroughs in superconductivity research may have a far-ranging effect on chip design and manufacturing.

NEURAL NETWORKS AND INTELLIGENT SYSTEMS

Some of the most exciting and promising research today is in the area of cognitive science and computer systems. Cognitive science seeks to understand how people learn; neural network research seeks to understand how computers can be taught to learn, in order to construct self-modifying, intelligent systems. Work in this area combines psychology, neurobiology, and computer science. Particular applications of neural network research may help to build intelligent natural language processing and voice recognition systems; image processing and pattern recognition; and expert systems.

NATURAL LANGUAGE PROCESSING AND VOICE RECOGNITION

Computer scientists, working in tandem with linguists and psychologists, are trying to make it possible for people to speak directly to computers as they do to one another. This involves teaching the computer to recognize and process ordinary human speech. If perfected, natural language processing will free the user from having to learn a special computer language. Systems exist that can respond to a limited vocabulary of voice commands, but the day when we speak to our computer in the same way we speak to our friends or fellow workers is still some ways in the future.

IMAGE PROCESSING AND PATTERN RECOGNITION

Many of the projected applications of advanced computer technology depend on teaching machines to "see"—that is, to recognize and identify shapes and objects and respond to that visual input. Advances in robotics and automated manufacturing, for instance, are tied to developments in this area. Again, some advances have been made. Digital processing of images is fairly advanced. Still, much work remains to be done before computers will be able to see and process images in anything that approaches our own ability.

EXPERT SYSTEMS AND KNOWLEDGE ENGINEERING

Expert systems are software packages that incorporate facts about a subject and a human expert's ways of interpreting those facts. Researchers in expert systems distinguish between *data* and *information*. Data are raw facts: your body temperature, heart rate, and rate of respiration are data. Information gives meaning, significance, or value to raw facts. The knowledge that a body temperature of 104°F is dangerously high is information. Expert systems combine this information into a knowledge base and guide the processing of program input according to "rules of thumb" or *heuristics*. These rules of thumb are supplied by human experts and built into the software. Knowledge engineers specialize in the construction of these complex and difficult programs. They work closely with scientists, physicians, or other experts. Some observers believe that knowledge engineering will be a powerful force in the future. They argue that many decisions made today by people will eventually be made by expert systems.

One exciting potential of expert systems research is that it provides a way for exceptional human knowledge and experience to be recorded, shared, and passed on to others. The expert system gives its creators a kind of immortality. Moreover, the knowledge of many experts can be pooled to build a system that surpasses the ability of any single human expert.

MULTIMEDIA AND HYPERMEDIA

Advances in computer graphics, compact disk storage, and other audio-visual systems have led to an interest in exploring the combination of sound and image reproduction with computers. The Media Lab at the Massachusetts Institute of Technology is a leader in this area. At the Media Lab, computer technology is joined with video and audio technology to create new kinds of learning systems, entertainment systems, and artistic expression.

HUMAN-COMPUTER INTERACTION

An important area of research involves making it easier for people to interact with and use computers. Applying the methods of traditional human factors engineering, as well as newer methodologies, researchers in the field of human-computer interaction design the *user interface* of the computer system. Specialists in this field may work on the design of hardware or software. Mice, graphical windowing systems, the use of icons in place of text, voice input systems—all are the result of user interface research.

WORKING FOR A START-UP

A start-up is a small, new company developing a new product. The rewards for working at a successful start-up can be enormous. Many of the wealthiest people in the computer industry—not to mention the world!—earned most of their money in start-ups. The excitement of working on a new product, the greater control and responsibility one usually has in a start-up, and the more intimate working atmosphere of most start-ups can be almost as attractive as the potential monetary rewards.

A start-up can also be a disastrous venture for all concerned. For each start-up that succeeds, many more quietly fail, leaving their employees without jobs. Managers in a start-up are sometimes less experienced than managers in more established companies. Benefits may be thinner, and there may be less sensitivity in dealing with personnel issues. Still, the potential rewards for working in a start-up are enormous, and experience gained even at a failed start-up can prove useful throughout your career.

Start-ups usually offer salaries that are lower than those for equivalent jobs in established corporations. Employees may also be expected to work longer hours. The physical surroundings and equipment may be more spartan than at a large corporation. To compensate for these inconveniences, employees in a start-up usually receive options to purchase stock in the company.

Since the start-up's stock is normally not traded on a stock exchange, the options actually have no value until one of two events occur. Either the company "goes public," offering its shares to investors on a major stock exchange, or the company is purchased by another entity, which pays all shareholders for their stock. Neither of these are likely to occur until the start-up ships a successful product and begins making substantial profits.

While start-ups usually have few true entry-level positions, their often thin financing leads them to value talented and energetic young engineers and programmers. If you are considering working for a start-up, you might want to ask these questions:

1. How much experience do the founders have in business? Have they ever run a successful business before?
2. How do the experience and skills of the technical leads stack up?
3. How is the company funded? That is, where does it get the money to pay your salary? If it is venture funded, how long can the company operate before it becomes profitable?
4. How comfortable are you with the risks of working for a start-up? How will you feel if the company fails or lays you off due to a lack of funds?
5. How much of your time and energy are you willing to commit to your job?

MARKETING AND SALES

Marketing

Marketing in the computer industry falls into three categories: product marketing, corporate marketing, and marketing sales support. Product marketing managers are concerned with marketing a specific product. They analyze the market potential for that product on the basis of the four classic marketing tools: product definition, pricing, distribution, and promotion. Product marketing managers determine how a product looks to the customer. They may be involved in manufacturing decisions, planning the product introduction, and working with advertising, creative departments, and public relations. Product marketing managers will also work with customers to guarantee that the product meets their needs, and with the sales force to help them sell the product.

Corporate marketing includes business planning, competitive analysis, forecasting of industry trends, and a variety of other tasks. In large companies, the corporate marketing group, managed by a vice-president of marketing, may include marketing communications, advertising, market development, and vendor relations. Corporate marketing staff usually have business, rather than technical, degrees.

Marketing sales support includes a broad range of programs that help the field sales force sell, support, and maintain the company's products. This group often serves as a liaison between sales and product groups. They may develop product demonstrations, applications, or training programs used by the field. They may also work with large accounts in conjunction with the field sales representative. Marketing sales support requires technical skills and knowledge of a company's products. Thus, it can provide a good transitional position for someone with a technical background who wants to move into marketing or sales.

Sales Representatives

Sales representatives (or "sales reps") sell computer hardware, software, and systems. They work for vendors selling mainframes, midrange systems, personal computers, special-purpose computer systems, and software. They sell software and peripheral equipment like printers, modems, and telecommunications interfaces. The sales representative links vendor and customer, matching customer needs with vendor products.

With the cost of computer equipment declining and the range of applications extending, the need for sales representatives is increasing. In addition, customers increasingly look to sales to provide support, training, and customization services.

To become a sales representative, you need a thorough understanding of computer hardware, software, systems, and applications. You must also be able to judge the customer's needs to provide an appropriate system. Sometimes the customer organization will know their own computing requirements. Sometimes, however, the rep must start from scratch, working with a client who may know little about computers to define computing needs and select an acceptable product. Thus, the sales representative depends on his or her communications skills. Oral communication skills are particularly important, as the sales representative often makes informational and sales presentations and must talk easily with clients. In addition, the sales representative must be energetic, highly motivated, and willing to travel. Most computer sales occur at the customer's site. The sales representative travels to these locations to demonstrate a product or close a sale. Many sales reps work on a quota system. This means they are responsible for making a certain number of sales within a limited period of time, usually on a quarterly basis. Compensation for sales reps is generally tied to performance. A sales rep may receive a base salary, supplemented by bonuses based on his or her sales.

The successful sales representative must have a certain flair for sales. One industry recruiting expert describes this as a "sales personality," difficult to define, but clearly recognizable. Computer sales does not, however, employ stereotypical high-pressure sales tactics. Sales representatives in the computer industry believe in their product and can back up their belief with technical knowledge. Large sales may be the result of bids or proposals prepared by the vendor and its sales representatives in response to specifications supplied by the purchasing organization. Most clients spend a considerable amount of money to purchase computing systems; they are paying in part for the expertise of the vendor's sales personnel. Moreover, clients are sometimes highly sophisticated computer users and expect sales representatives to spell out in detail all technical features of the products they are selling.

Education varies among sales representatives, though most jobs with larger vendors require a college degree. Some engineering-oriented vendors, especially those that sell to technically sophisticated users, prefer to hire people with a computer science or engineering degree, if they show sales potential.

Other companies look for individuals with a marketing or other degree and some evidence that they can deal effectively with the technical features of the products they will represent. Some college programs provide training in technical marketing and sales.

In either case, a company's sales force will be exhaustively trained in the company's products. And training is an ongoing part of the sales representative's job, as new products are developed or present products modified.

Sales representatives generally move into marketing or sales management positions. District managers supervise the sales force and direct the sales operations for a particular geographical region or handle one or more special client accounts. District managers are promoted to regional managers.

A degree in computer science combined with marketing and sales experience and an MBA is a virtually certain ticket into executive positions. Sales representatives also may find opportunities to move into managerial positions with customer companies. Having worked to supply the customer with the best system, sales reps have learned the customer's computing needs from the inside out. This knowledge and their experience with the system that they sell make such individuals attractive employees to customer organizations.

Sales opportunities also exist with retail computer stores. Most of these positions do not require a college degree in computer science. Many may not require a college degree at all. Management of retail computer stores takes more specialized computer training combined with business education.

Technical Support Representatives

Technical support representatives provide a liaison between a vendor's sales force and the organization purchasing the vendor's system. Systems engineers focus on software problems, while field or customer engineers specialize in hardware. Before a sale, technical support personnel evaluate a customer's computing needs. They demonstrate equipment or software, help to write sales proposals, and generally assist the sales representative to deliver the system that best meets the client's specifications. After a sale, technical support representatives install the system and get it up and running. Their responsibilities do not end here, however. Technical support representatives continue to serve as consultants to their clients. They may train users, resolve problems that arise in day-to-day use of the system, and function as troubleshooters. When something goes wrong, the user contacts the systems engineer for help. IBM pioneered the idea of such continuing customer service and has set the standard for marketing and sales support for the entire computer industry.

Technical support representatives are salaried members of a vendor's technical staff. Unlike sales representatives, they may not work on a commission or quota basis. Clearly, though, these individuals play an important role in the sales function. While the sales force may sell the system, the technical support representatives ensure that it does what it is supposed to do. The reputation of a vendor is often based on the adequacy of its field technical support.

Most vendors prefer to hire technical support representatives who have a four-year computer science or related technical degree, although some marketing personnel may move into this area if they develop enough skill in handling technical problems. Technical support representatives must be flexible enough to learn about the client's businesses in order to understand their computing needs. And because so much of a technical support representative's job involves talking with their customers and giving presentations, excellent oral communications skills are necessary, as well as the ability to adapt to the customer's environment.

Technical support representatives usually undergo extensive training in their company's hardware and/or software, and in other subjects important for developing workable systems, such as networking and telecommunications. This training will involve marketing techniques and communications strategies as well. After training, a systems engineer is assigned a number of client accounts, and spends most of his or her time at customer locations. Field engineers are called in on an as-needed basis.

A company's "personality" and expertise is reflected in its technical support staff. These positions are a good choice for the individual who wishes to work with people as well as with systems. Moreover, work in technical support offers the immediate reward of seeing the usefulness of your work when you help your client to use your system effectively.

Advancement opportunities from technical support can lead to either management or technical positions. From technical support, some people will move into sales, and advance to manage marketing and technical support activities. Those who enjoy the technical challenges of this job will advance to advisory, senior, or consulting levels in systems and customer engineering.

CHAPTER 3

WORKING FOR EVERYONE ELSE

While it is true that most of the "leading edge" work is done by computer vendors, the greatest demand for employees comes from the business world. The most powerful and impressive effect the computer has on contemporary life is the degree to which it makes more information available, to more people, and more quickly than ever before. The computer also provides tools that allow people to search, organize, and use information in entirely new ways. The computerization of the financial world, for instance, has profoundly affected the ways we access, spend, and invest our money. Automated funds transfer, automatic tellers, and up-to-the minute computer processing have changed the ways we interact with banks. The stock and bond market has also changed profoundly as a result of computerization. Many experts believe that a major stock market collapse that occurred in October 1988 was triggered by computerized trading. Entirely new kinds of financial instruments have evolved that would not have been possible before the computer.

The use of computers and information technology has changed the very structure of American corporations. The old hierarchical model, with many layers of management, was suited to the organization of mass production. Today, information is a company's most vital resource. The computerization of businesses has led to flatter management structures, organizations in which the management and analysis of information are critical to corporate survival. You can work in this new organizational context if you choose to apply your technical skills to solving business problems. In this chapter, we turn to the opportunities that can be found helping organizations develop and maintain their information systems.

EMPLOYERS AND ENVIRONMENTS

Most employers may be classified as either business, government, or non-profit. The kind of employer you work for can have a profound effect on the course of your career.

BUSINESS

Business is the largest source of computer-related jobs. The atmosphere is likely to be more competitive than in the other groups. There can be more risk and less security due to acquisitions, mergers, downsizing, and a changing competitive environment. At the same time, businesses often pay more than other kinds of employer. Raises and promotions in the business environment are usually based on performance, and opportunities for advancement may be more plentiful than in a government or non-profit setting.

It is worth mentioning that both government and non-profit institutions frequently turn to business for computer technology. By working for a government contractor, or for a computer-related business whose customers are non-profits, you may be able to enjoy some of the intangible benefits of non-profit or government work, while still earning a competitive salary.

GOVERNMENT

Promotions in government are based more on seniority and less on merit than in business, although there are many exceptions to this generality. Because government positions generally pay less than positions in private enterprise, there may be less competition for some positions that entail a lot of responsibility. A government job may offer you the opportunity to use your computer science expertise on large and important projects, in areas such as social security, the military, air traffic control, and space travel.

Government positions are usually more secure than jobs in the private sector. Many fall under a form of civil service regulation, which can provide important protections for workers while also restricting to some extent the opportunities available for promotions and raises.

NON-PROFIT ORGANIZATIONS

The non-profit employment sector is vast. It includes most educational and health-care institutions, as well as an infinite variety of advocacy, political, charitable, and religious organizations.

Working for a non-profit can be much like working in business, but it can also offer non-monetary rewards that are uncommon in the business world. In the educational environment, you might contribute to advanced research or gain satisfaction from teaching. In other non-profit positions you may experience the rewards of helping others. It is hazardous to generalize about such a diverse sector, but jobs that offer the greatest intangible rewards will often have a lower pay scale than similar positions in private industry.

CORPORATE SOFTWARE DEVELOPMENT

Corporate or "in-house" developers design, code, test, and debug the applications that help their company perform its business functions. They may help to design overall information processing systems and to organize the ways that information is handled and processed within an organization. Banks and other financial institutions; accounting, real estate, and insurance firms; credit card companies; and personnel, payroll, and accounts departments of every kind of business: all employ corporate developers.

Many positions in business data processing are identified by the title programmer-analyst. This job title can mean different things in different companies. In small companies with small computers, programmer-analyst may be the main job category, even at the entry level. This reflects the fact that the computer person in a small business may have to do just about everything related to the company's computing system.

This person will do routine programming. He or she will also design, maintain, and supervise all aspects of data processing operations.

In other situations, the title programmer-analyst represents the growing recognition on the part of businesses of the importance of systems analysis and systems integration—that is, getting the best software and making it work most effectively. This is especially true as more companies purchase their business applications software from commercial vendors, making changes or providing input to fit their own requirements. Since the main program is purchased from others, a company needs fewer in-house programmers to do basic programming tasks. What employers seek are programmer-analysts able to analyze software requirements, select the best available system, and make sure it works as well as possible. In business data processing today, systems analysis and systems optimization occupies a growing amount of the computer specialist's time.

Finally, in large companies, the title programmer-analyst may be little more than an indication of status: a level of promotion above the entry-level category of programmer.

Corporate developers still do some of their work in COBOL, a programming language designed in the 1950s to solve problems in business data processing. Many business applications are based on commercially available spreadsheet and database products, however. On PCs, and in distributed networked environments, corporate developers use tools such as Visual Basic to customize desktop applications like Microsoft Word, Microsoft Excel, or Microsoft Access. They may work with client-server tools, such as Borland Delphi or PowerBuilder, to connect desktop PCs to corporate databases. Or they may build applications from the ground up using C++ or other object-oriented programs.

Successful corporate developers combine a knowledge of business applications tools with a background in accounting, finance, or other business-related subjects. If you are considering this field, you should take business courses in college and might want to consider a business minor. Indeed, many employers hire those graduates with accounting or other business degrees who have a good knowledge of computing and information systems. You might also want to consider a college major in information systems (IS) or systems sciences, rather than in computer science.

To do well as a corporate developer, you need excellent interpersonal skills. You will often have to talk with people in many different departments of your company. You may have to instruct and supervise others, especially if you work in a smaller company. And you will certainly have to provide management with the succinct, easily understandable reports they expect.

As a corporate developer, you typically begin as a programmer-trainee or beginning programmer, if you work in a larger organization. You advance to chief or senior programmer, programmer-analyst, systems analyst, and into information management. It is not unusual for successful individuals to move into senior management positions. People begin as programmers; for the most part, they do not remain at this level. But for the right kind of individual, business applications programming is an excellent place to start. More opportunities are available in this field than to any other group of computer professionals. And openings exist in virtually every industry.

SYSTEMS ANALYSIS

Systems analysts solve problems and design systems to improve the efficient handling of information, people, materials, and machines in business and industrial settings. The Association of Systems Management, the major professional organization in the field, defines systems analysis as:

> ...the process of reviewing the information and operational flows within an organization as a basis for service to management. It contributes to the optimal operation of the organization via two avenues: information systems to provide timely, accurate, and meaningful information to management for use in decision making; and operating systems to accomplish specific organizational functions.

Systems analysts look at an area of a company's operations that is wasting time, causing trouble, or costing too much money. Employing various analytical techniques, including cost accounting, sampling, interviewing, and computerized model building, they define the problem, come up with a solution, and report their proposed improvements to management. In this capacity, systems analysis is akin to operations research (see chapter 5). While systems analysts work closely with computers, they are really systems, not computer, specialists. That is, they use their computer expertise to study and improve a department, process, or situation that they conceive of as a system, or interconnected series of conditions and events.

An example will help us better understand systems analysis. Let's say that a company would like to improve the way it deals with the information that flows through it each day. A systems analyst will see this flow of numbers, names, and words as an information management system. He or she will study current methods of dealing with this data. What information is needed? Who needs that information? Which employees are needed to handle this information? What kind of computer hardware and software is available? How much is the present information management system costing the company? Is it cost effective? The systems analyst will ask these and many other questions before arriving at an assessment of the system. Then he or she will design a different system to improve the efficiency and lower the cost of information management. This might be a set of specifications describing appropriate software, input data, the way data is filed and stored in the computer system, and system output. It would also probably include the procedures or methods that employees should use in optimizing the system—that is, getting it to perform as efficiently and economically as possible.

Systems analysts work in industrial and manufacturing environments as well as in business. In this sphere, a systems analyst is similar to an industrial engineer. For instance, a systems analyst may look at a factory and discover there is a problem in the flow of raw materials that is slowing down production. To solve this problem, the systems analyst would come up with a method to guarantee that enough materials are on hand to keep the plant operating at its most cost-effective level of productivity.

As you can see from these two examples, systems analysts are generalists. They may find themselves working in a variety of areas within an organization. They might work in accounting and finance departments, in administration, purchasing and inventory control, manufacturing and production, sales and marketing, even personnel management. To solve problems in manufacturing, a systems analyst must know something about production. To improve productivity in the payroll department, he or she will need to have some grasp of the principles of accounting.

Systems analysts combine their knowledge of computer languages and systems with practical knowledge of the area in which they work. An ability to learn, a breadth of knowledge, and a store of practical experience are important keys to success in systems analysis.

A recent advertisement for a position with a large manufacturing company gives a good idea of the many facets of the systems analyst's job. The company was looking for an individual who could:

- Write programs to process order, sales, billing, cash receipts, and sales reports and to forecast marketing trends
- Analyze business procedures and problems to refine data and convert it to programmable form
- Confer with heads of individual departments to determine their information needs
- Study existing data handling systems to evaluate information processing effectiveness
- Develop new systems to improve work flow and production
- Manage projects, assist in writing proposals, and perform feasibility and cost analysis studies

The majority of systems analysts are employed by manufacturing and processing companies, banks, financial or insurance organizations. Some work for consulting firms or system integrators. Systems analysts also work for public utility and transportation companies and for the federal government.

What kind of education does systems analysis require? Systems analysts must be familiar with programming languages, computer concepts, systems analysis techniques, and data retrieval techniques. Preferably, they have an undergraduate degree in computer science or information systems. A few colleges offer undergraduate degrees in systems analysis. Some systems analysts have a degree in business supported by significant college coursework in computer science. Additional training in finance, banking, insurance, or other fields related to the kind of company for which the systems analyst works is considered desirable. For this reason, many systems analysts complete a fifth year of study beyond their bachelor's degree in a business-related subject. An MBA can be an additional asset to a career in systems analysis.

Few, if any, individuals will begin their career as systems analysts. Most systems analysts begin as programmers, advance to programmer-analysts, and are promoted to systems analysts after some time on the job. This may take several years. Indeed, most systems analysts are over 30 years of age and have been employed in computer-related positions for a number of years. This experience gives them a good understanding of the overall functioning of their organization. This overview is necessary if the systems analyst is to see company operations as a system of interdependent units.

As well as being well paid, systems analysts have many opportunities for advancement. Senior and lead systems analysts work with clients and management; they supervise other systems analysis staff as well as programmers and other information management personnel. They may advance to become manager of systems analysis, supervising all systems-related projects within an organization. Advancement into information systems management is also possible. These management positions can lead to the highest levels of company responsibility.

Advancement in systems analysis is based on an individual's on-going education in the latest information technology and resource management techniques. In-house training, seminars and special courses offered by computer vendors and professional organizations, and reading professional publications help the systems analyst to stay informed about new developments. Success in systems analysis demands a high level of professional commitment.

EDP AUDITOR

EDP (electronic data processing) auditors are the watchdogs of large data processing systems. EDP auditors help their companies reduce financial losses attributable to data processing operations and guard against future losses. Working in banks, large public accounting firms, and other financially based businesses, EDP auditors assess computer systems and data processing procedures to locate any possibility of loss and evaluate the degree of risk involved.

EDP auditors locate irregularities, errors, and fraud in information processing systems. These errors may be something as innocent as a typing mistake or hardware malfunction. Errors of a graver nature are the EDP auditor's target as well. Unacceptable accounting methods, unauthorized access to computer files, or outright fraud are detected and reported to upper management.

About three-fourths of an EDP auditor's time is spent collecting information. The auditor interviews information processing personnel, administers questionnaires to system users, checks the computer programs to find errors or potential problems in coding, and verifies that all information on file is correct and up-to-date. Other duties may include advising management in the selection of a data processing system or special software package to suit company needs, testing new systems to make sure everything is working reliably, and writing programs to audit the system. The EDP auditor is like a police detective; he or she makes sure that no one is siphoning off a few cents here or there into a private account.

Clearly, an EDP auditor must be able to program well and must fully understand computer operations. He or she will have a broad background in business applications programming, and will have worked on a variety of systems. In addition, a good EDP auditor must understand accounting and financial practices and keep up-to-date on the latest auditing techniques.

Communication and interpersonal skills are exceedingly important to an EDP auditor. He or she must often report unpleasant facts to upper management and has to be able to talk with programmers, accountants, and other information systems personnel about what they do without arousing their defensiveness or antagonism.

To become an EDP auditor, you need an undergraduate degree in computer science or in business with considerable computer coursework. You also usually need at least two years' experience in the design, programming, and operations of large business systems. An MBA degree or certification as a CPA (Certified Public Accountant) is an added qualification.

A position as EDP auditor offers motivated individuals who have advanced to senior programmer or systems analyst positions an opportunity to move into management. Work in EDP auditing can lead to higher-level corporate management or to consulting.

Database Manager

The database specialist builds and maintains a large, cross-referenced library of computerized information using a special kind of software, called a *database management system* (DBMS). A database can integrate a number of separate files, making information instantaneously available to users. For instance, in a large health clinic, a variety of information must be kept on each patient. The clinic keeps records on personal statistics: the patient's name, address, date of birth, marital status, number of children, and so on. The billing department needs to know the patient's name and address, as well as all visits to clinic physicians, and the charges for those visits and other services. The dermatologist needs records of the patient's office visits, diagnoses, and treatments. He or she may need to know that the patient visited the allergist two years ago for treatment of a skin rash, but there is no reason that the doctor should have to deal with information on billing and payments for that visit. If each department or doctor maintained separate files, a great deal of information would be unnecessarily duplicated. This would take considerable computer memory space. Moreover, if each user of the system had to extract the information on, for instance, visits to the allergist from facts on all other aspects of the patient's records, much time would be wasted.

The database specialist designs a software system to combine these records into a single, efficient data structure (or system of files), and makes sure that each department can quickly retrieve just the information it needs. In other words, the database specialist is a kind of resource police officer, managing information and making sure the database is both usable and useful for those who need it. In smaller organizations, the database manager (sometimes called a database administrator) may have no staff or budget. In larger operations, a database manager may supervise other database programming specialists and will work within a budget allocated for information management.

Database specialists get the essential information to the users who need it, and keep unauthorized users from retrieving confidential or classified data. In some installations, database specialists may be in charge of overall computer security.

The demand for database specialists is expected to grow, especially as more and more organizations seek to use the vast amount of information they have collected to improve their ability to compete in the marketplace. American Express, for instance, sorts the information in its customer database to tailor special promotions that reflect the spending habits of small groups of customers. Magazines use database marketing to create custom editions with advertising targeted at sub-groups of subscribers. Other trends that support the need for database specialists include "data warehousing" and the increased use of executive information systems (EIS). Data warehouses are custom versions of the much larger version of a company's information, information that could be spread over many different sites. A data warehouse brings the data together for a specific use, often by EIS software. Executive information systems allow company management to look at and compare many different factors—sales, prices, inventories, and customer calls, to name only a few—so that they can make more informed business decisions.

Database specialists work in large companies. They are also employed by companies providing information management services, and in consulting.

To become a database manager, you need several years of technical and business data processing experience and an expert knowledge of data structures, programming languages, and operating systems. Advances in expert systems may create a new kind of information manager, responsible for constructing and maintaining dynamic knowledge bases. At this point, the "resource police officer" becomes a knowledge engineer.

Director, Information Systems

The IS director is an executive who spends most of his or her time directing all aspects of information systems and processing within an organization. Advancing from systems and information management positions, the IS director hires and supervises systems and applications programmers, systems analysts, and other personnel. He or she assesses overall information processing needs and makes recommendations for system improvements. The IS director is principally responsible for budgeting for data processing staff and operations. He or she writes proposals and reports concerning improved systems operations and answers to high-level management.

The IS management position is itself at a high level within an organization. Achievement of this position represents many years of management experience. Although most information systems managers start their careers as programmers, by the time they arrive at this level of management, very little of their time is spent in direct computing activities.

In larger organizations, an individual is promoted to director of IS only after gaining considerable experience in systems management. Because decisions made in the way information is handled and processed can have dramatic effects on a company's productivity, the IS manager must know a good deal about the particular industry in which he or she works. Large organizations look for job candidates with technical and business skills, and tend to favor the candidate with an MBA.

OPERATIONS

The operations staff works in a computing or information center to keep the computer system running and applications software available. It is hard to make generalizations about computer operations because so much depends on the size of the installation. In a small facility, one college-trained individual may be responsible for every aspect of computer operations. In large computing centers, the staff can be sizable, with a resultant range in job titles and specializations. Personnel can include junior, senior, and lead computer operators, peripheral equipment operators, hardware technicians, job-control clerks, data entry staff, librarians, shift supervisors, and a technical support staff—all overseen by an operations manager.

Operators keep track of computer operations and networks. Operators coordinate the flow of jobs through the system. They mount and dismount the tapes or disks that store programs, input, and output, and make sure that all equipment is operating smoothly. When something goes wrong, operators attempt to restore normal operations or notify the person in charge of troubleshooting—usually the operations manager. Because operators know their system so well, their description of breakdowns can be essential in returning the system to working order.

Hardware technicians service and maintain the PCs, other computers, printers, modems, drives, and other equipment. Most computing and information centers also have a librarian or librarians to catalogue and file magnetic tapes and disks, keep this material in good condition, and retrieve it as it is needed for specific jobs. Program librarians are responsible for cataloguing and maintaining programs. Sometimes program librarians will work as members of a programming team to keep track of sections of code as they are written and record the status of testing, debugging, and completion of each piece of software.

The technical support staff maintains systems software and deals with any problems that can be traced to that software. They may also write customized programs for special purposes. In addition, they talk with end-users to make sure their applications programs can be run effectively.

People working in computer operations were once considered the manual laborers of the computer world. Jobs were low-paying and offered limited opportunities for advancement. It is still true that many of the routine jobs in computer operations do not require a college degree or specialized training. Today, however, operators, operations managers, and members of the technical support staff are all expected to have a high degree of technical knowledge and experience. This generally translates into a college degree in computer science or a computer-related subject.

Computers run 24 hours a day, seven days a week. Operations personnel work in shifts and on weekends. This makes part-time jobs or internships in operations very attractive for students, who can schedule work around their classes. And the practical experience gained working in operations will make your coursework much more understandable and relevant. It is an excellent way to learn about the machines. Also, employers look favorably on computer science graduates with such down-to-earth experience.

Computing or Information Center Operations Management

The manager of a computing or information center directs and oversees all aspects of computer operations. His or her main responsibility is to keep the computer—peripheral equipment, data communications system, and software—in good working order. In other words, the operations manager works to keep the system running smoothly, efficiently, and without error.

The operations manager almost always works in mid- to large-sized organizations, such as hospitals, universities, banks, or large companies. Most operations managers work with mainframe and minicomputers in large-scale database and communications-oriented environments. They are in charge of all aspects of the system and staff, including scheduling, quality control, and maintenance of systems and some applications software. To do this, they supervise a number of people in the machine room and on the data processing center staff. They also work with users or the managers of user departments to provide the facilities these departments need. In a university computing center, for example, the operations manager may need to guarantee that the system provides output to the admissions office, the registrar, and the payroll and personnel divisions. At the same time, the system may be used by professors involved in research that requires computing and by students for instructional purposes. A large system must be many things to many users. The operations manager coordinates these diverse demands on the system and ensures that it functions for all purposes and all users. In smaller installations, the operations manager's responsibilities are much the same, although the size of his or her staff and the range of system applications are more limited.

The operations manager is part supervisor. He or she also must be able to communicate with users who may know relatively little about computing. Nonetheless, this job remains essentially technical in nature. The operations manager works with the machines. He or she must have a high level of hardware, operating systems software, and data communications expertise and a good deal of practical experience with large computer systems. This job also takes a certain amount of psychological resilience, for the operations manager must answer for any problem in the system. In the final analysis, when something goes wrong and the system goes down, it is the operations manager's problem.

Technical Support Services Management

The technical support staff is responsible for maintaining the operating systems software of an intermediate to large computer center. Technical support groups also develop and maintain special-purpose software, such as the telecommunications and database management programs that link remote computers and peripheral equipment to the central system. The manager of the technical support group supervises systems software programmers, schedules work, assists in troubleshooting, and takes part in planning and evaluating the overall system. If additional hardware or software is being considered, the technical support manager will be involved in the purchase decision. He or she also talks with users who are having problems running their applications programs on the system and with vendors of systems software packages to find out what might be causing a particular problem and how it can be fixed.

To become the manager of a technical support group, you need considerable experience in systems support. Commonly, the manager is promoted from within the support group staff. You must be willing to supervise and account for the work done by your staff and be acutely aware of the technical niceties and limitations of your system and its software. This position is not one for people who are easily frustrated, as discovering the reason for a glitch often takes all the skill and patience of a master detective, as well as an almost intuitive understanding of the system. For those problem-oriented, creative systems programmers, though, who want to stay in primarily technical positions, technical support management is a good career goal.

The proliferation of personal computers and growing use of local area networks (LANs) to connect these computers has had a profound influence on corporate information management operations. Information centers (info centers or ICs) are now charged with providing many different services. Info center staff members may evaluate and recommend software and hardware products, and may help decide which products an organization will select as standards. They may be responsible for end-user support—that is, helping users understand and use their spreadsheet, word processor, or other programs. They may install, configure, and help to maintain software for other employees, or serve as the local area network administrator. Info center employees may customize software for use within their organization. They may provide education and training services. And in some cases, info center personnel may serve as "beta" users to test new software supplied to them by vendors.

INFORMATION SYSTEMS DEPARTMENTS

Programmers and programmer/analysts in most information systems departments are guided by project leaders. Groups of specialists in documentation, communications, and database management may also be directed by supervisors. Groups of these sections may be headed by a manager. For example, there may be various sections of programmers and programmer/analysts for different products, services, or areas. The people in computer operations, operating on different shifts, may report to a manager.

In addition to these continuing leadership positions, temporary project leaders are often selected to head project teams in developing new systems or revisions or phases thereof. Such teams may have several programmer/analysts and programmers, one or two users, and a network database or other specialists if needed. Since corporate development projects typically have a beginning and end, assembling project teams as they are needed has become a practical way for designing, coordinating, and testing new and revised systems.

The head of all of these information systems functions may be called the chief information officer, or CIO. More and more, this officer is a vice-president or senior vice-president. It is this officer's role to plan how information systems can best serve the needs and interests of the organization and to direct the whole information systems organization to that end. In this role, the CIO must work closely with the top executives of all activities of the organization to see that their individual needs are well served by the information services department.

SYSTEM INTEGRATORS, VARs, AND CONSULTANTS

Elsewhere in this book, we talk about the trend towards "outsourcing" many information systems projects. Companies outsource to consulting companies because they find it more economical, or because they do not have the technical expertise the project requires. Also, an outside consultant may bring fresh insights into the way a company operates that employees may overlook or take for granted. Small businesses do not have the luxury to hire their own computer professionals; they, too, turn to outside sources to develop, install, and maintain the systems they use to run their operations.

System integrators, VARs (value-added resellers), and consultants all offer services to large and small companies. System integrators (as the name suggests) focus on integrating the wide range of hardware, networking software, and applications that a company may use. System integrators may also resell equipment and software as part of their services. VARs provide many of the same services for their clients, although a larger portion of their income generally comes from sales and support, rather than from consulting services. Consultants primarily sell their time and knowledge, although some may also resell products. As you can see, these titles overlap to provide many of the same services.

Consulting organizations range from large traditional accounting and management consulting companies such as Andersen or Price Waterhouse to small local firms with only a handful of employees. Some consultants offer a broad range of information systems practices; others focus on specific areas of expertise like risk management, network integration, or application development. Increasingly, large corporations will assemble teams made up of representatives from more than one consulting organization to address a particular problem.

Working with clients requires well-developed interpersonal skills. You are often working at your client's site and serve as an ambassador for your company. In some cases, you may be responsible for writing proposals, making sales presentations, and—as your career progresses—negotiating the scope of work.

Working for a consulting firm, VAR, or integrator can have many advantages. The larger international consultancies such as Andersen or Price Waterhouse offer a certain prestige, coupled with an opportunity to develop your technical skills in a highly charged environment. You learn about your clients' business needs and help them resolve problems or improve the way they operate. Working for smaller firms provides an opportunity to work at a variety of customer sites and on many different kinds of project. In many cases, you will be able to see clearly the positive results of your work.

GOING INDEPENDENT

Not all high-tech professionals hold full-time salaried positions. An increasing number work as independent or quasi-independent contractors. This trend is especially evident in software development and software testing. Contractors give up the security of a full-time job for the higher pay and greater flexibility of working on a hourly basis or by the project. They work for computer vendors, as well as for other businesses and in other industries.

Contract work is usually not an option for new graduates in computer and technical fields. Because contractors are more expensive on an hourly basis than permanent employees, managers prefer to hire someone who has demonstrated the ability to perform the kind of work required, instead of hiring someone who can learn on the job. Some companies hire contractors directly, while others hire through contract recruiters. Contract recruiters make their money by charging the company a percentage of the contractor's hourly rate; it is never necessary for the contractor to pay the recruiter for anything. In some cases, the contractor is actually an employee of the recruiting company for the duration of the contract.

Although contractors earn more per hour than most permanent employees, they receive none of the benefits usually associated with full-time employment. Contractors do not receive vacation pay, paid holidays, or paid sick leave. Contractors must arrange their own health insurance and retirement plans. Because the employer or client withholds no taxes from contractors' pay, contractors must calculate their own estimated taxes and pay them on a quarterly basis. Some companies spend considerable sums on continuing education for their employees, yet contractors must spend their own money to keep up-to-date.

Contractors also must look for a new job far more frequently than most people who work as permanent employees. A contract might last as little as a month or as long as a year; most are in the three- to six-month range. Between contracts, contractors have no income at all and may need to spend a great deal of time and effort searching and interviewing for a new contract.

Despite the disadvantages, contracting can be highly rewarding. Working on many projects for different companies contributes to the richness of a contractor's experience and provides a broader view of the industry. Contractors who work on an hourly basis are paid for all hours actually worked, unlike salaried employees who sometimes may feel exploited when they are asked to work long hours without additional compensation. And it can be satisfying to be in control of one's own business, however small it may be.

CHAPTER 4

FIVE CAREER PROFILES

In this chapter we look at five individuals who have launched successful careers in computing. Each person talks about the rewards of a computer career, and each has advice that will be useful to those just starting out. This chapter will give you a sense of the range of opportunities available to you and suggest where you might best apply your skills.

OPERATING SYSTEMS PROGRAMMER

Although Rob received his B.S. in computer science barely five years ago, he has an impressive 15 years' experience in computing. He was introduced to computing at 14, writing programs in BASIC in his junior-high computer lab. He was not impressed. "If BASIC is all there is to computers," he thought, "there's nothing special here: anyone can do it." At sixteen, Rob learned PASCAL. This was something else. As he says, he "started fooling around and did things I shouldn't have." In the process, he wrote a small calculator program. At this point he says he became "addicted to computing."

Rob was fortunate enough to attend a large metropolitan high school with a special program in computer science. He spent three to four hours a day playing with computers during his last two years of school. At 18, Rob landed his first full-time job as an operator/programmer at a construction company. He was able to pay for his college education through a series of jobs in computer programming and operations, working full-time in his senior year in college.

After graduating from college, Rob accepted a position as a systems programmer for a major computer vendor. He developed special in-house systems management programs for that company's own computing needs, then joined a product design team. Rob wrote about 80 percent of the software for the new product—a specialized microprocessor. He recalls that, like many design projects, this did not flow smoothly from concept to prototype to production. The first circuit board the team came up with proved faulty; the circuitry had to be redesigned. Eventually, though, the microprocessor was completed. Today, it is sold throughout the United States. Rob describes the special satisfaction that completing a project of this sort gives: "It's a neat feeling when you see something you worked on very hard make it to market and be liked."

Today Rob is part of the technical staff of a telecommunications company. His job title is manager of the operating systems group for desktop workstation products. Rob joined his present employer because he wanted to work on products that would more directly affect the people who use them. As a microprocessor designer, Rob was working with embedded software, or *firmware:* that is, programs that would be built into the microprocessor itself and never be seen by users. Today, he works on programs that people see and use directly. This fits well with his belief that computers are about helping people and making their lives easier.

Rob's daily responsibilities include minimal management duties supervising a small team of operating systems programmers. He is principal systems architect for the operating system design of a new personal computer communications product.

Rob thinks that computer science is slowly becoming a true science. From his own experience, he will tell you that it is a very worthwhile science to approach. But his emphasis is on the word *science.* Students considering the field are warned not to limit themselves just to programming. Rather, Rob feels, they should take every opportunity to learn as much as possible about the underlying principles of the field. Additionally, as someone who hires other computer science graduates, Rob advises those interested in research and development to obtain a master's degree in computer science. This, he feels, is rapidly becoming the standard base-level degree for work in R&D, while the B.S. degree typically leads to applications programming positions.

ENGINEERING PROGRAMMER, HARDWARE DESIGN TEAM

Scott is a technical person who is in the process of directing his career toward management. He works for a computer vendor as an engineering programmer. In the evenings, he takes courses at a local university and is working towards his master's in business administration (MBA). His employer encourages and pays for this additional education.

Four years ago, Scott received his B.S. in computer science from a large public university. His minor in engineering technology gave him hands-on training in electronics. This practical experience has proved very useful to him in his present position as a member of a hardware design team.

In Scott's experience, a typical design project has three phases. First, there is a brainstorming period where the team decides what they want to do, what technology is available or needs to be created to get the project done, and where the market will be when their new product is ready to be released. Next, specifications are developed that outline the step-by-step procedure to be followed to convert an idea into a real product. Scott says that at this stage, the team is working out "what goes on in the black box we're creating." This leads to the technical blueprint, or engineering specifications, that the team will use in their work. During the third and longest phase of a project, Scott says, "We roll up our sleeves and start getting the product out—hardware, software, documentation." A short project might last eight months. On average, most teams work together for eighteen months to two years.

Scott is good at what he does. He enjoys what he describes as "a feeling of satisfaction that you can go from point A—the specifications—to point Z—the final implementation—and get the whole thing working properly." Why, then, is he working on his MBA? In part, because he sees only limited possibilities for advancement. He feels that there is only so much need for "technical horsepower." And this need can be met by each year's crop of college graduates who do the real "grunt work" on a project. Not everyone will carve out a special place for themselves as a technical "guru" in any company; for many, the technical path is not, as Scott sees it, extremely realistic. The more likely path to advancement leads to management. And as a realist, Scott knows that an MBA will enable him to move up in his company. Or he can use his technical and business knowledge to start his own consulting business. For the time being, the knowledge he gains from his business courses continually improves his daily job performance.

Scott firmly believes in the relation of practical work experience and formal education. He recommends that students in computer science "get experience as soon as possible." Experience, he says, will help you find out what you want to do. It helps you learn "what this nebulous term 'programming' is, and how it relates to you" and your interests. He suggests cooperative education programs, summer jobs, or part-time work in computer operations on your college campus as good ways to gain experience.

APPLICATIONS PROGRAMMER, SOFTWARE DEVELOPMENT

Sharon had planned to become a research biologist, but on her way towards a degree in biology she got sidetracked by computer games. As a result, she is now a developer for an industry leader in business productivity software.

Although she was born in the United States, Sharon attended high school in Jerusalem. In Israel, high school students select major fields of study, just like college students in the United States. Sharon majored in biology. When she graduated from high school, she wanted to attend college near her sister, who lived in the Boston area. And after attending an urban high school in Jerusalem, Sharon was looking for a campus in the city, so she selected Boston University.

Her first semester at BU was something of a disappointment. After the hands-on, research emphasis of her biology courses in high school, Sharon was less than enthusiastic about the way biology was taught at

BU. Bored with her chosen field of study, Sharon spent more and more time playing games on her PC.

Sharon decided to take a computer science course the second semester of her sophomore year. Of her first course, Introduction to Computer Science, she says, "It was easy, and it was really fun. It was the way my brain worked." She discovered that programming rewarded deductive reasoning: "My logic is pretty good," she says, referring to the way a program is designed. "If you understand concepts, you can figure things out."

On the basis of that one course, Sharon decided to change her major to computer science. "It was really pretty obvious," she remarks about this sudden change of career plans.

Sharon went on to take all the core coursework in the BU computer science program, as well as a number of computer-related electives. One of her most interesting courses, she says, was Computer Creativity. The professor teaching the course was affiliated with the Center for Advanced Visual Studies at the Massachusetts Institute of Technology. The course covered topics like graphics, video, and holography, as well as artificial intelligence and expert systems.

To complete this course, Sharon designed and implemented an intelligent computerized tourist guide to Boston. It let a visitor ask questions about the city in ordinary language, like "Where is the Museum of Science?" or "When was Paul Revere's ride?" The program supplied the answers, and even included a map of the local transit system, with directions to major attractions.

Because she had changed her major, Sharon spent a fifth year at BU in order to complete all the requirements for the computer science program. She was also able to plan time during her fifth year to work part-time, helping a woman physician at Boston's Dana Farber Institute organize her research records and grant proposals using an Apple computer.

After graduation, Sharon spent a few weeks in California, working to automate her brother's law practice using IBM PCs. Returning to Boston, she began her search for a first job.

Sharon decided to work with a "headhunter" and went through a number of less than satisfying interviews with a disk manufacturer, a PC clone maker, and other hardware-oriented companies. She talks about the way that, as a job candidate, you can intuitively sense that you're not at the right kind of company. Of one interview, in particular, she says she knew "right away" that "it wasn't the right job, and I didn't want to work for this company."

A good headhunter—one who makes an effort to find out your interests, work style, and career goals—can be an invaluable resource in finding the right job. Many people develop a strong loyalty to such individuals and will turn to them when it's time to hire others. But in this case, Sharon's headhunter continued to send her to interviews that were not in line with her own job objectives. Sharon knew what she wanted to do, so she began the interview process on her own with a company she wanted to work for. But the process was slow, and Sharon turned to an agency to find temporary work.

The first company the agency sent her to was the company she works for today. The job opportunity was in quality assurance (QA), not product development, but Sharon accepted the offer anyway because of a number of positive factors: it was a first-rate company, she liked the people, and she'd be working on the Macintosh computer. In other words, there was a "fit" between what the company offered and what Sharon was looking for.

Sharon's work involved testing the more technical aspects of a new Macintosh product, including communications and spreadsheet functions. This gave her an opportunity to demonstrate her technical competence. At the end of the project, the product manager, knowing that Sharon wanted to work on development, issued a challenge: if she could produce the code and technical documentation for a specific task he assigned, he'd move her into development. Sharon met the challenge, and went on to work as a principal developer for utility and personal information management products for the IBM PC.

Today, Sharon is back working on the platform she likes best, the Apple Macintosh, building groupware applications. She takes pride in her work, and contrasts her approach to "cowboy programmers who do and then think, rather than think and then do." Sharon looks at a programming task as a series of stages. First, she considers how best to do it. Then, she considers how what she does will affect other parts of the program being written by other members of the development team.

Only then does she begin to write the code. She also plans for quality by scheduling more time than she thinks it will take to complete a program.

Sharon advises those who want to work as developers to get experience while in school. "Get any development experience you can," she says. Otherwise, unless you graduate from a prestigious school like MIT, "you may find yourself in a Catch-22 situation, without enough programming experience to get the job you need to get that programming experience."

She also is quick to caution against taking a job you don't feel right about. At the same time, she will tell you to "Accept a job that may not be the exact job you want, if it's at a place you want to work. Be willing to start out doing something different."

If you're not yet sure you want to pursue a career in computers, Sharon will ask you to look at how you feel about programming: "You have to enjoy it to do it well," she remarks. "Sometimes it's surprising people pay you to do it."

SYSTEMS ENGINEER, MARKETING TECHNICAL SUPPORT

Cindy graduated three years ago with a B.S. in computer science and went to work for IBM as a systems engineer. In looking for a job, she felt she wanted to do something that would involve contact with people. She didn't want to spend all day sitting alone at her desk. Systems engineering, the technical side of marketing at IBM, offered her this opportunity.

Her first year at IBM was spent in intensive training. She was assigned to an advisor in a branch office of the company's marketing division, and worked with her advisor on small projects in order to gain experience with customers. At the same time, she completed self-study modules which prepared her for more formal training. These self-study courses covered technical subjects, including virtual storage concepts, distributed networks, and systems programming, all related to IBM hardware and software. Cindy was also becoming familiar with IBM equipment.

Every six to eight weeks during this year, Cindy was sent to three- to four-week formal training courses, returning each time to her branch office. This training included lectures on technical subjects and exercises designed to help her practice making sales calls and presentations. Cindy recalls that these training episodes were similar to the kind of work she had done in college. And she also remembers her reluctance to speak before others. She vowed to complete her training without ever giving an oral sales presentation before the other trainees. Of course, she didn't manage to avoid this training in oral presentation skills. As a result of this training, Cindy has become a confident and effective spokesperson for IBM equipment and systems.

Today, Cindy manages seven customer accounts. Most of her days are spent away from her home office at customer sites. Like other technical support professionals, she has developed a "home" in each of her customer companies and visits each at least once a week.

Cindy's responsibilities include systems implementation and maintenance. She makes sure that her customers have a system that can handle their computing needs. When customers have a problem or need a special application, Cindy advises them on IBM products that could be useful to them. Her main job is to keep their systems running smoothly. She deals only with software problems, however. When a hardware problem comes up, she calls on IBM's customer engineers.

Although she works, as she puts it, "in the trenches" with her clients, she is not paid on commission, as IBM marketing representatives are. She sums up her relation to the sales force: "The marketing representative makes the promises. We try to make it happen."

Cindy enjoys the many benefits of working for a large corporation. She sees many possibilities for advancement in both technical and management directions. IBM, she feels, has a basic "respect for the individual" and encourages an attitude that each employee is important in his or her own right. Because of this emphasis on individual worth and accomplishment, Cindy believes that IBM is a very good place for women. Employees are treated equally and without bias; advancement is based solely on ability.

Cindy enjoys her work tremendously. "I was interested in being technical, but not in being a programmer," she says. Her work as a systems engineer lets her use her technical knowledge and her skills with people. However, the pace of her job can get hectic: "I never run out of things to do and people to talk to." And IBM's commitment to new technology and product development means she never stops learning. As a new product comes out, she is one of the first to understand it and make it work for her customers.

For students interested in a computer career, Cindy agrees with other professionals on the importance of gaining practical work experience. She advises students to search out any kind of part-time or summer "hands-on" experience.

Cindy also suggests that a minor in electrical engineering would be a useful complement to the software emphasis of many undergraduate programs in computer science. Coursework in electrical engineering "lets you know how a computer works, from the inside out, and you cease to see it as a black box." Cindy's own undergraduate training emphasized programming skills. She feels that this helped her to "think like a computer—in a logical way," but points out that there is much more to computers and computing than programming languages. "Everything today is communications, databases, networking," she concludes. "If I had to do it over, I'd take tougher courses in computer *science*," not just programming.

MIS MANAGER

Bob, who has 15 years experience in the computer field, is the information systems manager for a small oil and gas exploration and production company. He got into computing, he says, by accident. Bob majored in accounting in college. One day, one of his accounting professors assigned a lab which required some programming. And that was it: Bob fell in love with programming.

Completing that assignment led Bob to a part-time programming job while he was still in school. And although he went on to complete his degree in accounting, he's been in the computer field ever since.

Bob has followed the classic career path. Once out of school, he was hired as an entry-level programmer. He advanced through the senior programmer level to become a systems analyst, then moved up into data processing management. Along the way, he obtained an MBA to increase his knowledge of management techniques. He has stayed in the oil and gas industry throughout his career, working for oil field equipment companies as well as oil and gas production companies.

Because Bob works for a fairly young, small company, he was solely responsible for setting up the entire information handling installation. In order to develop a system that would meet current as well as future needs, he interviewed top management to ascertain their information requirements and the overall company direction. He supervised installation of the system and continues to maintain and improve it. He hires (and fires) systems and applications programmers and programmer/analysts, and oversees the information processing department. About 80 percent of system processing involves general maintenance of company operations: payroll, accounting, general ledger, financial planning, and—because his company owns or leases oil-producing lands—software that keeps up-to-date land management records. The remaining 20 percent of company computing is devoted to processing seismic information, well logging, and other geological data related to oil exploration.

A good deal of Bob's time and energy are spent on budgeting for his department: a task, he points out, that is never completed. He also helps to acquire, install, and maintain new software systems as company information processing needs evolve. He spends hours on the telephone and in meetings, and admits that while he gains considerable personal and professional satisfaction from his management position, "frankly, programming is more fun."

Bob advises students in computer science to think twice about aiming for management positions. "Bit twiddlers" and "byte benders," people who are really excited by low-level programming and the machine, may not enjoy being a manager. Such people will probably be happier and more productive remaining in a purely technical or engineering environment as a systems programmer, project leader, or in scientific and engineering applications.

In hiring, Bob likes "to find the people who discover by accident that they have a flair for computing." He looks for young people who "like to play with computers" but also have some knowledge of business, "because they can talk with users." Bob sums up his advice to people considering a career in computers:

> Go to college and don't quit until you're through. At least get your bachelor's degree. And try to get some practical experience during college. It's extremely difficult to break into the field as a programmer-trainee. Only the very big companies can afford to train people.

CHAPTER 5

SPECIAL OPPORTUNITIES IN COMPUTER-RELATED FIELDS

Career opportunities in computer-related fields are increasing every day. We cannot begin to review them all in this chapter, but we will examine a few of the exciting opportunities that may await you.

DOCUMENTATION: TECHNICAL WRITERS

Technical writers combine a knowledge of computers (or other scientific or technical field) with an ability to write effectively. In the computer industry, technical writers provide *documentation,* the reference and users' manuals and other documents that support and explain computer products. This information may be in printed form or may be stored electronically as part of the software. Such an "on-line documentation" or help system has become standard. Documentation helps the user, who may know little about computers, to understand and use hardware and software applications.

Many fields, including aerospace, manufacturing, and government, as well as all areas of engineering, need individuals who can communicate specialized information to many different types of readers. Because of the spectacular growth of computer use in the workplace and the home, writers of computer documentation are in considerable demand.

People who begin their careers as technical writers may advance into managerial or administrative positions directing a technical writing group or publications department and coordinating document production.

Employers are always eager to hire individuals with good communications skills. In a competitive job market, the applicant who can communicate effectively has a clear advantage. If you would like to combine your interest in computers with technical writing, you should take as many courses in journalism and English composition as you can. Courses in technical writing and editing and in publications production are especially recommended. Many colleges now offer graduate programs in technical writing; some even offer undergraduate specializations in this field.

The Society for Technical Communication (815 15th Street, N.W., Suite 506, Washington, DC 20005) is the professional organization for technical writers and documentation specialists. This organization is a good source for additional information on this subject.

EDUCATION

Many opportunities in computer education exist within private industry and in public and private schools at all levels.

Vendors of computer hardware and software employ instructors to conduct in-house training and to teach those who purchase their products how to use them. For many vendors, customer training is central to their sales effort.

In-house company course instructors develop curricula and lead seminars and training sessions for employees and customers. These individuals often have advanced technical knowledge and the ability to share it with others. Customer training personnel combine their technical know-how with well-developed interpersonal skills. Oral communication and teaching abilities may be more important in customer training than advanced technical training. Thus these individuals may not hold college degrees in computer science. They may move into customer training from technical writing, technical support, marketing, or sales positions.

Depending on the company and its customers, training positions may require considerable travel. Certainly, to do well in customer training, you must enjoy helping others to master basic aspects of computer use.

Large companies often have an educational services department or division. In addition to coordinating all aspects of company training programs, this division may produce instructional materials, such as interactive tutorials on CD ROM, instruction guides, videocassettes, or films. Increasingly, companies are outsourcing training to other companies who specialize in technical education.

In public and private education, opportunities to teach students how to use computers exist at both elementary and secondary levels. Many public school districts hire specialists to assist them in bringing computers into their classrooms. In many schools, computer literacy is already an established part of the curriculum. And through computer-aided instruction (CAI), the computer can become a tool for teaching other subjects. CAI software has been written to teach everything from elementary arithmetic and spelling to advanced courses in fields as diverse as engineering fundamentals, foreign languages, and the anatomy of the brain. Instructional software has also been commercially successful with home computer users—and their children! The widespread availability of multimedia computers has fueled the market for "infotainment" and educational titles.

At the college and university level, the shortage of qualified computer science professors is severe. Three factors have brought about this shortage: the rapid growth in the number of computer science departments and degree programs, increases in student enrollments, and the fact that, on the whole, qualified individuals can make more money in industry than they can at the university. As a consequence, most computer science departments are hard-pressed to meet their staffing needs.

If college teaching is not always as financially rewarding as working in industry, it offers satisfactions of other sorts. College instructors introduce students to the study of computers, encourage their interest, and help to educate them to become productive professionals. They teach students from a variety of majors to understand how computers work and how they influence society. In addition to their teaching, professors conduct research and publish their results. For many professors of computer science, the chance to do research is extremely important. And many others supplement their incomes through consulting. The flexible schedule of the university gives them time for research and consulting.

College instructors must hold graduate degrees. A Ph.D. in computer science is preferred, although because of the present demand, many instructors are employed with just their master's degree.

MEDICINE

The potential for computer applications in medicine is extraordinary. At present, neither the nature nor extent of what computers might be able to do in medicine is fully known. There is still considerable potential for growth in straightforward data management applications: billing, patient records, the day-to-day recordkeeping of a hospital, clinic, or private practice. A major problem of most hospitals is making sure their bills are paid. The cost and quality of health care affects us all, and the pressure to keep costs under control is great. Automating medical records and billing has already improved health care productivity.

However, management of business information is not the only or most interesting way computers are used in medicine. Database software and computer networks provide physicians with instant access to information on poisons, rare diseases, and accident treatment. Information service providers, such as CompuServe or America Online, let anyone access abstracts of the latest medical research.

Even more intriguing possibilities exist in the development of systems that incorporate the knowledge of a doctor's lifetime medical practice. One such system, CADUCEUS, jointly developed by a physician and a computer scientist, diagnoses disorders and diseases in internal medicine. Another more specialized system, MYCIN, diagnoses blood and meningitis infections and suggests treatment methods to the attending physician. These systems not only assist experienced doctors and nurses, but can be used by medical practitioners in rural or remote locations where doctors are not available.

Computers have even been used in the area of mental health. One historical program, ELIZA, introduced in 1967, asked patients questions about their feelings, registered the pattern of words in the patients' responses, then formed new questions based on those responses. PC products that let you act as your own therapist also exist. This computerized feedback technique has proved remarkably successful, as many people find it easier to express their troubles and anxieties to a computer than to a human therapist.

Bioengineering—engineering applied to develop sophisticated technology to test and treat health problems—also relies increasingly on computer technology. We are all already familiar with simple devices like digital thermometers and blood testing equipment. We are also seeing daily advances in genetics and genetic engineering. In the future, computer science and engineering, bioengineering, genetic engineering, and robotics will combine in ways that even the most imaginative science fiction writer cannot conceive of today.

Both the Association for Computing Machinery and the IEEE Computer Society have special interest groups for medical computing. The American Association for Medical Systems and Informatics is also concerned with medical computing.

INFORMATION SCIENCE

Information scientists use their knowledge of computers and information processing techniques to design large information storage and retrieval systems. These systems let users obtain specific information from computer storage easily, quickly, and reliably. For instance, a geologist doing research on earthquake activity in southern California can instruct these systems to locate all information published on this subject in the past five years. The rapid expansion in human knowledge made possible by the computer has made information science a field of considerable importance.

Information scientists develop methods to collect, organize, and classify information for computer storage and retrieval. They then construct, maintain, and update the system they have designed. Information scientists often specialize in particular fields, such as agriculture, medicine, education, or chemistry. This is because they must have some understanding of the information to be classified. Automated searches of stored information are done using key words or descriptors. Thus, the system must be designed and key words selected according to the logic of the field itself. Increasingly, systems are using intelligent front ends to filter and select relevant information electronically. Many of these products are available to business and professional users, not just librarians.

Information science is closely related to library science, for these large information systems are essentially vast electronic libraries. In fact, you can think of information scientists as the librarians of the future. Information scientists are employed wherever there are large quantities of information to be organized. Employers include commercial data banks and computerized information services, large corporations, and government agencies, including the Library of Congress.

The American Society for Information Science can offer more details about careers in this field.

OPERATIONS RESEARCH

Operations research (OR), also known as decision or management science, applies scientific principles to decision making. The OR specialist analyzes a problem, then uses the computer to mathematically or statistically model (or simulate) the effects of alternate decisions. By so doing, he or she seeks to discover the most suitable course of action. OR is used to determine how best to design, operate, or manage systems to optimize the allocation of resources and people.

OR specialists solve problems in production management, improve computer networks and telecommunications systems, and design mass transit systems. They work with man-machine interface problems, automation and robotics, land use and highway planning, financial planning and forecasting, medical decision making, meteorology, ecology, and in many other areas of modern life.

Whether their subject is a hospital, a company, a production line, or an electrical power grid, OR specialists view things as a system. When applied to manufacturing and automation, OR is a tool of industrial engineering. While similar in many ways to (and often overlapping with) systems analysis, OR is distinguished by its heavy reliance on mathematics and statistics, modeling, and computer simulation.

By its very nature, operations research is an interdisciplinary field. OR analysts hold undergraduate degrees in many different disciplines. To become OR specialists requires a strong quantitative background, including courses in probability and statistics, linear algebra, economics, and, of course, computer science. Some colleges offer undergraduate degrees in operations research or management science. Some programs in industrial engineering, systems analysis, or management emphasize OR methods. However, most work in operations research requires graduate study. Typically, a student with an undergraduate degree in math, computer science, management, or engineering will go on to specialized graduate study in OR.

The Operations Research Society of America can provide information about employment opportunities in this field.

INDUSTRIAL ENGINEERING

In industrial engineering, computers are used to improve manufacturing efficiency. Computer applications include numerical control, computer-aided design and manufacture (CAD/CAM), and robotics.

Numerical control machines have been in use since the 1950s and are very common today. These are machines like a lathe, dedicated to a single manufacturing task and driven by a computer program, originally stored on paper tape. One of the early recognized advantages of numerical control was the ease with which manufacturing specifications could be changed by changing the computer program, instead of resetting the machine by hand. This saved time and labor and increased the flexibility of the production line.

More recently, computer-aided design and manufacturing (CAD/CAM) have come into wide use. Computer-aided design (CAD) relies on very high-power, high-resolution graphics workstations and software that allow engineers to draw a part or product design on the video screen. This eliminates time-consuming drafting and redrafting of various stages of the design. When the design is perfected, it can be printed and serve as the basis for manufacturing specifications. CAD applications have been widely adopted in the automotive and electronics industries, as well as by architects and other designers.

Computer-aided manufacture (CAM) uses a hierarchy of computers to control many facets of the production process. At the lowest level, process control computers perform and monitor separate tasks in the production sequence. At a higher level, computers monitor and direct the entire operation. In fully integrated computer-aided manufacture (CIM or ICAM), CAD programs are directly "down-loaded" to lower level computers, and operations research models automatically optimize the production system from design to end-product.

The most highly publicized element of CAD/CAM is undoubtedly robotics. Robots, for all the mystique the word evokes, are really just extremely flexible computer-controlled machines. A numerically controlled machine can be programmed to different specifications, but it can still only perform one task. A robot, on the other hand, can be programmed to manipulate a range of tools or to perform a number of different tasks.

Robots are programmed using specialized "geometrical" languages that instruct them to move from point A to point B. Because the robot cannot deviate from these instructions, the workplace has to be set up with great precision. Parts must be located exactly where the robot has been programmed to expect them. If a part is even slightly out of alignment, the robot cannot find it.

This problem could be solved if robots could be programmed to see or feel, to recognize shapes, and to adjust to differing conditions. To do this, industrial engineers and computer scientists are working to develop robot sensations, especially vision. So far, limited results have been achieved. But the day when robots have anything approaching human vision is some distance in the future.

Industrial engineering and robotics offer many attractive career opportunities. People will be needed to design the manufacturing tasks that robots will perform, to design the workplace in which they operate, and to program the machines. If you are interested in engineering applications of computer technology and have some mechanical inclinations, you might consider industrial engineering as a career option. The Society of Manufacturing Engineers has a strong student program. This group can give you further information about industrial engineering, CAD/CAM, and robotics.

CHAPTER 6

EDUCATION AND TRAINING

This chapter looks at the education you will need to prepare yourself for a successful, productive career as a software developer or information systems professional.

The most common way to enter the software profession today is through completion of a four-year program in computer science or a related program such as business analysis or information management. This was not always the case. In the early days of computing, there were no college programs in computer sciences. Many of the early pioneers applied knowledge gained in other disciplines, such as mathematics, biology, or engineering, to the developing field of computer science. Others came to software from fields as diverse as art, printing, literature, and languages.

Even today, not all software designers have a computer science degree. In fact, the number of computer science degrees awarded in the United States actually declined from the mid-1980s through the mid-1990s—at a time when computer-related job opportunities expanded dramatically. There are several explanations for this apparent paradox. First, many colleges now offer majors in business and information management that combine a technical education with business skills. For many information systems professionals, it makes more sense to follow this path rather than pursue a strictly technical degree. Second, some major computer companies, such as Computer Associates, seek out students with liberal arts or other majors for entry-level positions in customer support and other areas. As the new employees learn more about the companies products and technologies, some of them will move into software development, quality assurance, or marketing. Other companies consider students with two-year degrees for some entry-level jobs, because they do not have to offer as high a salary as they would to a graduate with a bachelor's degree. Nevertheless, many companies still require a four-year technical degree as a condition of hiring.

The personal computer revolution has meant that many more people acquire programming skills on their own, while in school, but outside formal classroom training. Small start-up companies that develop new products are less concerned about a potential employee's credentials than whether he or she can write first-rate code. Many people who work in user interface design, multimedia, or Web page development do not have computer science credentials.

What is true for software developers is also true for information systems professionals. Advanced software development tools make it possible to produce software applications without writing computer code in a language like C or C++.

PREPARING FOR THE FUTURE

Your best bet to securing a well-paying job in software development and information systems is still to complete a four-year degree program in computer science or a related field. At the same time, keep the following in mind:

- Competition for good jobs with good companies is the rule. Employers will always prefer candidates with outstanding grades, related work experience, and in some cases, graduate study.
- Technical skills alone are not sufficient. Employers need employees with good written and oral communication skills. Indeed, information systems professionals say one of their major challenges is communicating with other employees for whom they are providing software and services. Your college program should include solid training in business and technical writing as well as oral presentations.

- Creative thinking is an important element of solving software development problems. If you pursue a technical degree, make sure to take advantage of any chance you have to take courses in non-technical disciplines that will help you "think out of the box."
- Technology changes rapidly. The skills you learn in college may be obsolete by the time you start your first job. As a software professional, learning new skills and mastering new information will be an absolute must. Your education will never end.

Finally, in today's world, most people will change careers not once, but two or three times throughout their working life. Keep this in mind as you acquire the education and training you need to enjoy a career in software.

Top executives in information systems are occasionally selected for their talent at understanding business needs, their ability to think creatively about how computer resources can be applied to achieve business goals, and their leadership skills at motivating the people they work with.

When the Association for Systems Management asked its members what they had specialized in college, they got some interesting results:

	No. of Replies	% of Total
Computer Science, Math	583	25
Business Administration	493	22
Accounting, Finance	301	13
Liberal Arts	274	12
Engineering or Science	230	10
DP, Programming	198	9
Other	213	9
Total	2,292	100
No reply	106	
Total replies	2,398	

The levels of education of the association members reported in this survey are also revealing:

	No. of Replies	% of Totals
No college	86	4
Undergraduate college—no degree	335	14
Undergraduate degree	859	36
Postgraduate college—no postgraduate degree	390	16
Master's Degree	657	28
Doctoral degree	61	2
Total	2,388	100
No reply	10	
Total replies	2,398	

These charts show that 82 percent of the association members reporting had an undergraduate degree or higher and that many, but not the majority, majored in computer-related subjects (computer science, math, and DP/programming). What this study reveals is that it is possible to enjoy a career in information systems or software without completing a four-year computer science degree.

LEARNING ON YOUR OWN

Regardless of whatever formal education you pursue to prepare for a software or information systems career, you can also learn a great deal on your own. If you or your family own a personal computer, you can increase your computer knowledge by writing your own programs using tools like Borland's Delphi or Microsoft's Visual Basic for Windows-based machines, or Apple's Hypercard for the Macintosh. There are many other software tools available that will let you explore and learn on your own. Also, users' groups abound. Participation in these loosely organized groups of enthusiasts is a great way to develop your software skills, as well as meet interesting, like-minded people of all ages and occupations.

You can also learn about computers and software by taking part in on-line forums, accessing information on the Internet, and reading books and periodicals.

HIGH SCHOOL

If you are still in high school, what can you do to begin to prepare for a career in computer science? We can offer you four points of advice:

1. Follow a solid college-preparatory course of studies with an emphasis on mathematics and English.
2. Learn as much as you can about computers and computing.
3. Develop good study habits.
4. Begin planning for college as early in your high school career as possible.

It is never too early to begin to plan for college. By the end of your junior year, you should be making concrete plans for your college education. If you have decided that computer science is attractive to you, you will want to read the following sections in this book on selecting a college. Choose four or five colleges you think you might like to attend, and write for copies of their catalogs, admission requirements, housing, financial aid, and other information. Most schools require that students submit their results on the Scholastic Aptitude Test (SAT). These tests are offered at a limited number of locations several times each year, and you must arrange to take them in advance.

In addition to standardized tests of academic achievement and ability, many colleges and universities have other admission requirements. You may need to have taken a given number of credit hours in English, social science, science, math, or foreign languages. Some schools will also ask you to write an essay explaining your reasons for seeking admission to their school. They may want you to visit their campus for an interview with a campus admissions officer or provide letters of recommendation.

If you plan to go to college, you should be enrolled in a college preparatory program in high school. Your coursework should include solid training in mathematics, especially if you are interested in the theoretical or engineering aspects of computers and computer science. Physics is also recommended. Good communications skills will be crucial to your success in college and beyond. Take as many English courses as you can, especially those with a strong emphasis on writing. A course in public speaking or speech communication will further improve your confidence and self-expression, helping you to communicate effectively with others.

Needless to say, you should take every opportunity to learn as much as you can about computers and computing. If your high school offers courses in programming, by all means take them. If your school has a computer club, you will certainly want to become a member.

Admission to the better colleges and universities requires good grades. A record of solid academic achievement will increase the likelihood of your acceptance by the college of your choice. Development of good study habits and a commitment to perform at the peak of your ability will encourage your academic success in high school. And good study habits and self-discipline will be essential in college. Writing and debugging programs, learning about computer science theory and practice—these things demand concentration, patience, attention to detail, and time. If you cannot discipline yourself to study intensely, and to set aside significant amounts of study time and use that time effectively, you stand little chance of doing well in college. Each year, numbers of college freshmen fail to make it to their sophomore year because they never developed good study habits while in high school.

TWO-YEAR JUNIOR AND COMMUNITY COLLEGES

Many two-year junior and community colleges offer associate degrees in computer-related studies. An associate degree may help you to obtain an entry-level job with some companies or small businesses.

However, most professional-level positions in computing require a four-year college degree. Certainly, you will enjoy better wages with a four-year degree.

Many students choose to attend a junior or community college for two years, for financial or personal reasons, and then transfer to a recognized four-year school. For many students, this is a good way to smooth the transition from high school to the more competitive university environment. It can also help students who decide fairly late in high school that they want to obtain a college education. A year or two at a junior college can give you time to improve your study habits and your grades and may better prepare you for more advanced study in computer science.

If you decide, for whatever reason, to attend a two-year college and to transfer later to a four-year school, it is important to follow a general course of study that will satisfy the requirements of the college or university to which you wish to transfer. Be careful to take a wide range of general requirements. A narrow emphasis on computer or technical courses may jeopardize your admission to the college of your choice. Also, many colleges and universities will not accept all credits transferred from another school. This is especially true of requirements in your major field. You will cause yourself the fewest problems and potential disappointments if you discuss entrance requirements and transfer policies in advance with admissions officers from your chosen four-year school. You will then be able to plan your junior college curriculum so that you meet those requirements.

FOUR-YEAR COLLEGES AND UNIVERSITIES
Selecting a College or University

In selecting a college or university, you should be guided by a number of considerations.

The strength of the computer science program. Factors to consider include the size and reputation of the program, the depth and variety of its curriculum, the professional standing of its faculty, whether any special programs or concentrations are offered, and its success in placing its students in interesting, rewarding positions when they graduate. Is the computer science department part of a college or school of engineering? Is it accredited by the Computer Science Accreditation Board (CSAB) or by the Accreditation Board for Engineering and Technology (ABET)? At smaller colleges or universities, or schools without an engineering division, how adequate is the computer science curriculum? Will your coursework include computer architecture, data structures, language theory, and systems and hardware? Or does the curriculum consist primarily of courses in programming languages?

Computing facilities. Do the college and its computer science department maintain a variety of computer equipment, from mainframes to personal computers? How easy is it for students to gain access to these facilities to complete labs and homework assignments? Are there enough machines to meet student demand? Is there a campus-wide network? Can you plug your own personal computer into that network to access campus resources?

The general reputation of the college or university. This can be reflected in part by the general prestige of a school, its national and local reputation, and the success of its alumni. You should also consider the breadth of a school's general curriculum (the best will offer a well-rounded education), the faculty-student ratio, and the average SAT scores of its students.

Location, cost, and availability of student loans and other financial aid. The relative importance of these factors will vary for each individual.

The campus. What are the overall characteristics of dormitories, classroom buildings and grounds? Is the campus attractive and well-maintained? Is security sufficient at urban campuses?

Other qualities. Many other, less specific qualities may enter into your choice of a college or university. Did your parents attend the school? A school's traditions, attitudes, and quality of life may influence your decision. Remember, however, that your first concern should be to select the school that will give you the best computer science education in the context of a good general education.

Many books are available that will help you to answer these questions and make an informed choice of a college or university. You may wish to consult one or more of the following:

- *American Universities and Colleges* (Washington, DC: American Council on Education)
- *Barron's Guide to the Best, Most Popular, and Most Exciting Colleges* (Woodbury, NY: Barron's Educational Series)
- *Barron's Profiles of American Colleges* (Barron's)
- *The College Blue Book* (New York: Macmillan Publishing Company, Inc.)
- *The College Handbook* (published by The College Entrance Examination Board)
- *Comparative Guide to American Colleges* (New York: Harper and Row)
- *Lovejoy's College Guide* (New York: Macmillan)
- *The Right College* (New York: Arco)
- *Peterson's Guide to Four-Year Colleges* (Princeton, NJ: Peterson's Guides)
- *Cass and Birnbaum's Guide to American Colleges* (New York: Harper Collins)
- *The Big Book of Colleges* (New York: Random House)

The College Handbook is also available electronically through America Online, giving you instant access to detailed information on all accredited two-year and four-year colleges and universities in the United States. Each entry describes admission policies, degrees offered, undergraduate majors, academic programs, academic requirements, application deadlines, student activities and services, annual expenses, financial aid policies, and more. You can also search the on-line *Handbook* for colleges that offer specific features.

You may want to consult *The Insiders' Guide to the Colleges* (New York: St. Martin's Griffin) for an honest description of colleges and universities written by students. This book goes beyond academics to give a good picture of everything—from dress codes to drug use.

Undergraduate Curriculum

The core of your undergraduate curriculum will consist of courses in computer science theory and applications. You can expect to be assigned many lab or homework problems that will require extensive time on the machines.

In addition to your classes in computer science, you will enroll in required and elective courses in mathematics, natural sciences, the humanities, communication skills, and the social sciences. You will probably take at least a few courses in another engineering field or in business. Courses in business will be especially helpful if you plan to work in corporate IS or as a consultant.

Mathematics is clearly an important field of study for computer scientists. Both the ACM and the IEEE Computer Society emphasize mathematics study. Mathematics will be especially important if you plan to work in scientific fields or in operations research. For others, courses in statistics are highly recommended.

Most colleges and universities have established science requirements for students in each major. The majority of engineering programs include four or five courses in general sciences. For the computer science student, physics is a clear choice. The fundamental laws of physics involved in electricity, electrostatics, electromagnetism, thermodynamics, mechanics, and even optics are central to understanding the principles of computer technology. In addition, you may want to consider courses in biology or biomedical sciences, especially if you are interested in the medical applications of computer science or in human factors and cognitive psychology. (Human factors studies the human-machine interface, that is, the way humans relate physically and psychologically to machines.) Linguistics, semantics, and formal logic can also be helpful in certain areas of computer science research and application. Physiology courses can be helpful in human factors study and in robotics and problems in human-machine information processing, as well as in neural network research.

The humanities include history, philosophy, literature, and the fine arts. Most colleges and universities require that students complete a number of humanities courses to ensure that their graduates are well-rounded, literate individuals. As a student in computer science, you may find courses in the humanities (and the social sciences) a refreshing change from your technical studies. Learning to appreciate art, literature, or music, and becoming informed about the history of human culture, will enrich your life in ways you will appreciate for years to come. Coursework in liberal arts may well prove useful, as well as interesting, if you aspire to management. Recent studies of the college background of senior executives show a strong correlation between achievement in the business world and a college education that stressed the liberal arts.

Like the ACM, the IEEE Computer Society recommends that computer science students take courses in writing and communications skills. Classes in technical writing, technical editing, and advanced composition (emphasizing practical rather than literary writing) will help you write functional specifications and market requirements documents, as well as help you document your code for those who maintain it. It will also make it easier for you to write all the memos and reports that are a necessary part of all professional jobs. Your specialized knowledge of computer science will be of little value if you cannot communicate it in an understandable way to those who need your expertise. Students interested in programming language theory, natural language processing, and artificial intelligence will find courses in linguistics and semantics useful.

In business applications, management, marketing and sales, and consulting, oral communication skills are essential. Courses in speech communication, including technical or professional speaking and group or organizational communication, will help you develop these skills. A better understanding of human communication strategies will enable even the most technically minded individual to work more productively as a member of a project team.

The social sciences include anthropology, psychology, sociology, political science, and economics. Most colleges require some coursework in these subjects. Psychology, especially cognitive psychology, will prove useful to students interested in artificial intelligence, pattern recognition, or human factors. Learning how the human brain can perceive and think can lead to better modeling of thought in machine applications.

For students interested in information systems jobs, economics courses are important. The study of economics will help you understand the fundamental principles underlying modern business and financial transactions and decision making. Banking and financial services depend on today's information technology; there is a good chance you will work for such an organization. Political science will give you a better comprehension of the ways in which economic and political structures are affected by computer technology. And a better understanding of political and economic forces will make you a more informed citizen of your country and of the global community.

In selecting engineering courses, choose courses that will be of service to you in the context of your career goals. If you are interested in hardware, drivers, and utilities, coursework in electronics, instrumentation, or control theory will supplement your work in electrical engineering. If you are interested in computer-aided manufacture and robotics, courses in advanced mechanics and industrial engineering are appropriate. A good advisor in your computer science department can help you to select these courses wisely. Coursework in data and telecommunications are also very important.

For those interested in business applications, systems analysis, or information management, study of accounting, finance, and management is important. You should also consider the option of enrolling in a degree program especially designed for business-related computing applications. These programs are variously called information science, systems science, or business analysis. Other degree programs emphasizing a range of computer applications in business and industry include systems analysis, systems engineering, industrial engineering, management science, and operations research. Most of these programs place less emphasis on the theoretical and engineering aspects of computers and more emphasis on practical problems of providing automated systems to do the work of business and industry.

Financial Aid

A college education is an expensive investment. In 1990, the College Board estimated the average annual cost of tuition and board at private schools to be about $10,000. At some of the more prestigious private schools, tuition was over $20,000. Today, in 1996, even state tuitions can top $20,000. While publicly funded institutions are generally less expensive, tuitions have risen dramatically across the United States. Furthermore, changes in government funding continue to make it more difficult for students to finance their education.

In addition to basic tuition and fees, you will need to pay for room, board, books, supplies, and incidental expenses. These costs mount up rapidly.

There is no doubt that obtaining a college education is worth this expense. A college degree is a ticket to higher-paying and more responsible jobs in many fields. A college education also gives you a rich foundation in cultural and historical knowledge that will enhance the quality of your life.

For many students, then, the question is how to finance that education. Many sources of financial assistance are available to help defray the cost of your college education. It is important, however, to plan ahead if you are seeking financial assistance. Begin *at least* a year before you expect to start college.

Types of financial aid include: 1) grants and loans based on a student's simple need; 2) grants and loans based on a student's (or a student's family's) ability to pay; 3) work-study programs; and 4) scholarships, grants, and awards made in recognition of a student's accomplishments or academic potential. Sources of financial aid include federal and state governments, foundations, civic groups, fraternal organizations, professional organizations, individual colleges and universities, and major corporations.

Many other sources of financial assistance are available, including state aid, college funds and scholarships, private scholarships, and employee tuition reimbursement programs. The following are a few of the many books that may help you finance your education:

- *College Financial Aid Annual* (New York: Arco)
- *The College Money Handbook* (New York: Macmillan)
- *Barron's Complete College Financing Guide* (Barron's)
- *Lovejoy's Guide to Financial Aid* (New York: Simon and Schuster)

- *Peterson's Paying Less for College* (Princeton, NJ: Peterson's Guides)
- *The Scholarship Book* (New York: Prentice-Hall)
- *Paying for College* (New York: Random House)
- *College Costs and Financial Aid Handbook* (The College Entrance Examination Board)
- *Barron's Best Buys in College Education* (Barron's)

Part-Time and Summer Employment

Many students help pay for the cost of their education by taking part-time jobs during academic terms or full- or part-time jobs during summers.

It is difficult to work more than a few hours a week and still have the time and energy to give your best efforts to your studies. And undergraduate programs in computer science are extremely demanding. Thus, many computer science students may find it hard to work during school terms. To do so and still do well in school takes self-discipline and, sometimes, an understanding, flexible employer. In considering working during school, be realistic in assessing your determination and your schedule. If you need or want to work while attending classes, make sure you are willing to sacrifice what little leisure time your studies may allow.

One kind of work, though, should be pursued wholeheartedly. Any computer-related work experience you gain during school terms and summers will be useful to you. The sensible computer student will seek out jobs in the computer lab or at the help desk. Such experience will increase the meaningfulness and relevance of your coursework. Moreover, employers seek out graduates with computer-related work experience in entry-level hiring. Computer professionals and employers are unanimous in stressing the benefits of this experience. Alternately, seek out opportunities to volunteer your services helping others to master aspects of computer and networking use. Many organizations will value this experience as much as on-the-job experience.

Summer vacations provide an excellent opportunity to obtain work experience and earn money to pay for college expenses. One way to find summer work is to talk to the computing center on your campus and to professors responsible for smaller computer labs. You can also contact local employers. Even a summer as a technician or as a sales clerk at a software store will give you valuable experience and a paycheck.

Intern or Cooperative Programs in Industry

Working in the computer industry during summers or as part of a cooperative education or internship program can give you valuable experience. You will gain a first-hand knowledge of the real-world work environment. And you will greatly expand your knowledge of computers and computing. Furthermore, many students who do well as interns or co-op workers receive offers of employment when they graduate.

Peterson's Internships lists those larger companies that hire students for summer work. You can also approach local employers of computer personnel. Your college placement office can often be of assistance. Your departmental advisor may also know of summer work opportunities or be able to tell you about intern and cooperative programs.

GRADUATE STUDY

For many individuals, graduate school will be an attractive option. There are a number of reasons why you may wish to seek an advanced degree. Some positions in research and development require at least a master's degree and, in some cases, a Ph.D. Individuals aiming for management positions, especially in corporate IS, will find that an MBA (Master of Business Administration), combined with an undergraduate computer science degree, will make them very attractive to employers. And a graduate degree in computer science, usually at the master's level, affords those with undergraduate degrees in other disciplines entry into the computer field. Finally, the Ph.D. is generally necessary to teach computer science at the college level.

The Master's Degree in Computer Science

The master's degree requires a minimum of 32 to 36 semester credit hours of study beyond the bachelor's degree. Some programs require completion of a thesis; others offer thesis and nonthesis options. You will, however, probably need to complete some kind of original research or programming project. You will certainly have to pass a comprehensive oral or written exam.

Two groups of people will benefit from taking a master's in computer science. First, if you wish to specialize in a certain area, such as computer architecture or software engineering, but are not ready or willing to commit yourself to a lengthy doctoral program, graduate study at the master's level may be your answer. If you are considering working towards a Ph.D., but want to test your aptitude and interest in graduate-level study, a master's program gives you this opportunity. After a year, you can leave academic study and take a job in industry or you can continue toward your doctorate.

A second group finds that the master's degree gives necessary proof of qualifications for employment in the computer field. These are people whose undergraduate degree is in another discipline, often in the liberal arts or social sciences. For these individuals, a good way to change the direction of their career is to obtain a master's in computer science, information management, or a related field.

If you are entering the computer field from another discipline, most computer science departments will ask you to successfully complete a number of undergraduate courses before admitting you to their master's program. This is necessary to give you the basic knowledge upon which your graduate courses will build. And it demonstrates to the department your ability to undertake more advanced study.

Before making a career change, it is best to enroll in one or two computer courses. If you do well and, more importantly, if you enjoy computing, then make plans to study for your master's if you feel it will enhance your job opportunities. But if you find you have to force yourself to program and to study, computer science is not for you. Find out first, before you make significant changes in your career goals.

Because the demand for skilled software professionals is high, if you can demonstrate a high level of technical knowledge and ability to produce results, a master's degree is not necessary. Employers look at what you can do to help their business succeed, not at how many degrees you have collected.

The Ph.D. in Computer Science

The Ph.D. requires more than 90 semester hours of study beyond the bachelor's level and the completion of a dissertation. It takes at least three years, and often longer, to obtain a doctorate. Doctoral study allows you to do original research in computer science and qualifies you to teach in colleges and universities and to perform advanced research in industrial settings or research institutions.

The Association for Computing Machinery annually publishes a *Graduate Assistantship Directory* listing grants, fellowships, and assistantships available in computer science departments throughout the United States. ACM also presents the Doctoral Dissertation Award for the outstanding dissertation in computer science and engineering entered in open competition.

CERTIFICATION

Many professions, such as law, medicine, or accounting, have certification procedures to ensure that their members are competent. There are no industry-wide certification standards for computer professionals. In fact, plumbers are subject to stricter licensing requirements than are computer professionals. However, the Institute for Certification of Computer Professionals (2200 E. Devon, Suite 268, Des Plaines, IL 60018) addresses this problem. The ICCP is a nonprofit organization established for the purpose of testing and certifying the knowledge and skills of computer professionals. Its constituent societies include most of the major professional organizations in the computer and data processing field. Certificates are awarded on the basis of tests administered twice annually at selected sites throughout the United States and Canada and overseas.

Certification is more meaningful outside than within the computer industry. If you plan to work in corporate information systems, certification can be a valuable credential. Few, if any, programmers working as software developers for hardware and software vendors have certification of any sort. In fact, among many of the best software developers, there is a concerted effort to counter government efforts that would place software professionals under the same kind of licensing to which professional engineers are subject to. Organizations such as the Computer Software Industry Association and the Software Forum have actively lobbied officials to prevent such a requirement.

COMPANY-SPONSORED EDUCATION AND TRAINING

Your education in software and information technology does not end when you receive your college degree. In many ways, it is just beginning.

For the first six to eight months you are on the job, you will be learning about company equipment, software, and procedures. This training may be formal or informal. How well you do during this initial period can affect your future success, as many employers see this as a probationary period.

Because of the rapid rate of technological change in the computer field, most larger companies offer many opportunities for the continuing education of their employees. Many sponsor both internal and external educational programs.

Internal training programs range from career improvement courses offered through the Human Resources department to seminars on specific technical issues. These courses may be supervised and staffed by the company educational services division or by outside consultants.

Many employers encourage their workers to go outside the company to further their education. Many sponsor employee enrollment in MBA programs to prepare technically knowledgeable people to move into management. An especially valuable benefit to you as an employee will be your company's tuition reimbursement program. In these programs, the employer covers the costs—tuition, fees, and books—as you work on an additional undergraduate or graduate degree. Any undergraduate seriously considering attending graduate school will do well to consider employment with an organization offering tuition reimbursement.

Some companies offer classes at their facilities taught by faculty from nearby colleges and universities. These courses may be general in nature, designed to improve employee productivity and professionalism. Subjects like public speaking and technical writing are popular. Some large computer vendors may even offer full undergraduate and graduate programs at their facilities in selected subjects.

Companies that invest in employee education consider their money well spent. Their investment pays off in better educated, more up-to-date employees, informed about advances in the computer field and better able to perform their jobs. A technologically obsolete employee is of little worth in a field as dynamic as computer science.

KEEPING UP WITH NEW DEVELOPMENTS

Because software and information change so rapidly in the information systems field, it is particularly important that you take steps to stay current with new developments throughout your career. There are many ways of doing this:

Read. Many magazines are available that cover most changes in hardware, software, and information systems management methods. Increasingly, these periodicals are available on-line.

Join a professional organization. Professional associations are another fine source of keeping up-to-date in an enjoyable way. These associations usually have monthly meetings in major cities, with speakers and seminars on topics of current interest to the members. They also have annual conferences of two or three days with leaders who are experts in their specialties. Most such groups have technical journals, which are included with membership.

Attend seminars. Many organizations conduct one- to five-day seminars in major cities on the latest technical subjects. These can often be helpful in becoming educated on a particular subject. They usually cost several hundred dollars, and most who attend have the seminars paid for by their employers.

Go to sales presentations. Vendors of hardware and software often put on demonstrations or classes as part of their marketing programs, and these presentations are a good source of information about the products covered. Check the business section of your local newspaper for information.

Go to trade shows. Trade shows and exhibitions are conducted in major cities in which many computer software, hardware, and services vendors have booths and exhibits displaying their products and services with marketing representatives to explain what their companies have to offer.

Go on-line. Subscribe to one or more of the on-line information services or Internet providers. A wealth of up-to-date information about computer hardware, software, and related topics is available on vendor Web pages on the Internet, on Compuserve, and on America Online.

CHAPTER 7

FINDING A JOB

What can you do to guarantee that you leave school with a promise of employment? How do you go about finding a satisfying job? What benefits can you expect? What questions should you ask before you accept employment? And how do you choose wisely among more than one job offer? These and related questions will be discussed in this chapter.

RESEARCHING EMPLOYERS

There are a number of ways to find out about potential employers and bring your qualifications to their attention. Job openings are advertised in newspapers and trade journals, and some general employment guides are published each year. You can write directly to a company inquiring about openings. And you can use personal contacts to get a foot in the door. Very likely, you may find your first job through campus recruiting efforts on the part of large employers.

In seeking a position in the computer field, your first stop should be the immensely helpful *Peterson's Hidden Job Market: 2,000 Fast-Growing Technology Companies That Are Hiring Now.* This guide lists employers who are hiring computer science graduates for positions in research and development, production, technical services, information systems and information processing, marketing and sales, and administration and finance. Each employer is briefly described, together with basic information on hiring needs, starting salaries, and the ratio of applicants to job offers. The name and address of the individual you should contact concerning employment is also provided.

You may also want to look at the *College Placement Annual,* an occupational directory listing information on positions in all fields customarily offered to college graduates.

Large employers of computer specialists sometimes obtain a list of graduating students from computer science departments or schools of engineering. You may receive a letter from such an employer (or from the United States military). By all means, apply for such a job if it is of interest to you. But do not expect too much. Companies who send out blanket invitations for applications are looking for very specific qualifications. It may be purely a matter of chance if your background exactly fits their staffing needs.

You can always contact a prospective employer directly, submitting a letter of application, together with your resume, that outlines your qualifications and interests. If it is convenient, you might also visit a company and talk with someone about the kinds of work done at that facility. Many companies will gladly talk to interested individuals about their work. Such informal contact can sometimes lead to later employment.

Your computer science professors may also be able to assist you to find a suitable position. Many professors maintain contacts with industry, and some work in industry as consultants. These individuals are often willing to aid students who they know to be well-trained, hardworking, and professionally motivated.

Your participation in student chapters of professional organizations such as the IEEE Computer Society or the Association for Computing Machinery may also help you in your search for employment. These organizations frequently sponsor guest speakers from business, industry, and the academic world. Not only will their presentations inform you of timely or significant subjects in the field of computer science, but guest speakers will usually meet informally with interested students before or after their presentation. The motivated student can make useful industry contacts, learn of openings in the speaker's organization, or learn about other companies that may be hiring computer personnel.

Another way to find out about potential employers is to join a computer users' group in your community. PC user groups are now found in almost every part of the United States. Through users' groups, you can meet other computer enthusiasts and exchange information and software. Many computer vendors send company representatives to give presentations at the larger user groups. These presentations give you additional information about employers and the products they sell.

In the rest of this section, we will cover the following methods of finding employment:

- On-campus recruitment
- Letter writing campaigns
- Responding to ads
- Using professional recruiters
- Technical job fairs
- On-line job resources

ON-CAMPUS RECRUITMENT

Many large companies in the computer industry send recruiters to colleges and universities with large or outstanding programs in computer science. In fact, many larger corporations such as Microsoft, IBM or AT&T may rely almost exclusively on campus recruitment to meet their entry-level staffing needs.

The campus recruiter will visit with qualified students interested in working for his or her company. These interviews are arranged through the school's career guidance and placement office, which will post or publish a list of companies scheduled to conduct on-campus interviews and set up individual appointments. Plan ahead if you plan to go through the campus recruitment process. You may have to sign up for interviews several weeks before the actual interview date.

The campus recruitment process allows companies to review a large number of job candidates quickly and easily. The on-campus interview gives you a chance to learn about the company, its work, and its policies. Campus interviews also give you an opportunity to practice your interviewing techniques.

On-campus interviews are basically screening interviews. Few, if any, job offers will be made. More likely, successful candidates will be invited, at company expense, to visit company facilities. During this "plant trip," you will spend a day talking to a range of company personnel and will learn first-hand what it would be like to work for that organization.

LETTER-WRITING CAMPAIGNS

A job-seeking broadcast letter campaign can be an effective, if tedious, way to secure the right job for those who may not have secured one quickly and easily through other means. The features of this type of campaign were developed by Carl R. Boll and described in his book *Executive Jobs Unlimited*. People who have used such campaigns have found them, properly done, to produce outstanding results. This technique is often used by people with a few years' experience who are looking for a new employment opportunity.

The principle behind these campaigns is to broadcast your talents and capabilities widely to those organizations within your areas of interest. By sending out a hundred letters or more, you are sure to hit a few who are looking for someone with experience like you and will ask you in for an interview.

The goal of a letter-writing campaign is to get job interviews. Characteristically, a hundred letters will achieve two to eight interviews, sometimes more. Playing the odds, one of three interviews normally results in at least one offer. And usually at least one of three offers is quite acceptable. So one hundred to two hundred letters should normally be enough to reach your objective. More can be sent in a slow period or if you are very particular in making your selection. One hundred a week is a good pattern.

Incidentally, it has been found that sending the same letter to the same list two or three months later achieves about the same percentage of interview requests. This reflects the fact that the needs and circumstances of companies do change.

The best type of letter to market your talents has been developed over the years by Boll and must be closely followed to be effective. The letter is addressed to the head of the organization or, at the lowest, to the head of the division where you would work—*never* to the personnel or human relations department. It consists of an introductory first sentence that expresses your best accomplishment statement. The second sentence says, "If your company (organization) wants a (title you seek), then you may be interested in other things I have done." This is followed by five to eight succinct accomplishment statements, each a paragraph of one or two lines long, each started with an action verb. The last sentence is something like "I would be happy to meet with you to discuss my experience in detail." Monarch size paper (7¼" × 10½") has been shown to attract greater attention and achieve better results than the usual 8½" × 11" size because it stands out from the bulk of other mail. A broadcast letter for George Schwartz, seeking a systems analyst position, might be written as follows:

GEORGE W. SCHWARTZ
1234 Evans Avenue
Washington, Rhode Island 43210
(213) 555-4321

July 6, 1996

Mr. John R. Irvington
Irvington Machinery Company
9876 Astor Street
Roosevelt, Rhode Island 54321

Dear Mr. Irvington:

As a programmer/analyst, I proposed simplifications which were adopted and reduced accounts payable action steps by 30 percent.

If your company needs a systems analyst, you may be interested in some of the other things I have done:

- Recommended computer scheduling change which cut downtime by 40 percent.
- Programmed an inventory control system in fifteen weeks that was scheduled for twenty weeks, or 25 percent faster.

- Completed coding programs for three new systems and two system revisions and assisted coding for three improvements.
- Stood in top 10 percent of my programming training class.
- Brought in twelve new members to Association for System Management's Lincoln chapter, as membership chairman.
- Majored in information systems at St. James University. Grade point average was 3.8.

I would be happy to discuss my experience with you in more detail.

Sincerely yours,

George W. Schwartz

This letter gives enough information for the prospective employer to tell if he or she has an interest in your skills. If so, your letter will be routed to the person who would actually decide whether or not to hire you. If you are lucky, you will arouse the curiosity and interest of this individual and will be asked to submit a resume, screened in an initial phone interview, and called in for an interview. If not, your letter will be routed to Human Resources where it will just end up in a file. At worst, your letter will go directly into the wastebasket. Because this is nearly a shot-in-the-dark method, do not be disappointed if you do not see quick results.

Developing the mailing lists for these letters can take some time. Addresses can be found in Dun and Bradstreet's *Million Dollar Directory* or *Poor's Register of Corporations, Directors, and Executives,* which are available at most libraries. Also, most libraries have state directories of commercial organizations.

RESPONDING TO ADS

Many software development and information systems positions are advertised in trade publications such as *Computerworld* and in the classified section of major metropolitan newspapers. The Sunday editions of the New York Times, the Boston Globe, and the San Jose Mercury

News have numerous listings, including many jobs that lie outside their geographic areas. National employers, such as Microsoft or IBM/Lotus, will advertise in these widely read papers. Most of the positions will call for experienced personal. Do not be overly discouraged by this. Not all companies that regularly hire recent graduates advertise entry-level positions.

Another rich source of high-tech job ads is *High Technology Careers Magazine* (4701 Patrick Henry Drive, #1901, Santa Clara, CA 95040; phone 408-970-8800). Published every other month, it features advertising from vendors in hardware, software, telecommunications, and the Internet. *High Technology Careers* is also on-line at http://www.careerexpo.com.

If you do find a position for which you are qualified, you must respond promptly. The earlier your response is received, the better chance you will have to be actively considered for the job.

Those who place ads in the major publications say they receive hundreds of responses to each ad, sometimes thousands. Most respondents send in a resume, possibly with an added handwritten or typed cover note. The statistical odds of receiving an interview are about a hundred to one. It is not a lot of trouble to send in resume copies to these advertisers, but the likelihood of receiving a position or even an interview that way is not very good.

Preparing tailor-made letter responses to advertisements dramatically improves the response percentages. Doing this, you can expect better response rate compared to the usual one percent. The approach that can achieve the favorable rate is by preparing a letter much like the campaign letter, including terse statements of your pertinent accomplishments. Include in the ad response letter those measurable results that relate to what the ad says the employer wants. Try to have an accomplishment statement for each qualification the ad calls for.

USING PROFESSIONAL RECRUITERS

The use of professional recruitment services is common in the software and IS job market. Personnel agencies and job placement firms are motivated to help you find the job you want because they collect their fees only when they make a successful match between a candidate and an employee. Technical recruiters—often referred to as "headhunters"—are contracted by potential employers to hunt down the right candidates. They can make sure your resume gets to the individual who makes the hiring decision.

Robert Half and Source/EDP are two nationwide personnel agencies that specialize in information systems positions. Robert Half is an older firm that handles financial, accounting, and information systems positions; it has offices in major cities throughout the United States.

Source Services is another nation-wide personnel agency, recruiting software and IS professionals. Source Services is the parent organization of Source/EDP and Source Engineering. Both of these services work to place software professionals. Source/EDP focuses on placing computer professionals in research, development, and, especially, MIS positions. It maintains regional branch offices in cities throughout the United States and Canada. Source Engineering is a professional recruiting firm devoted exclusively to the engineering field; it works to place both hardware and software engineers. Source Engineering has offices at locations where employment in the computer industry is concentrated, including California, Massachusetts, New Hampshire, New York, Oregon, Texas, and the Washington, D.C. area. The staff at Source/EDP and Source Engineering is made up of people who have worked extensively in the fields of computer science and engineering. Their own job experiences enable them to provide informed counseling, career planning, and placement services to other professionals. Source Engineering and Source/EDP publish yearly salary surveys that can be useful guides to the kind of compensation you can expect. The surveys also include helpful information on planning and evaluating your career growth. For more information, contact Source Engineering by mail at P.O. Box 7573, San Mateo, CA 94403-7573, or phone the Source Engineering or Source/EDP office closest to your location—or the location where you'd like to work.

Many other engineering and computer science employment agencies are located in major centers of the computer industry. When you work through such an agency, you'll work with a specific headhunter who will seek to match your skills with available openings in a variety of companies. Headhunters are an important link between a company's hiring needs and people looking for a new job. The best headhunters develop ongoing relationships with several companies and hiring managers. When a manager needs a new employee, he or she often turns first to a headhunter who has provided good employees in the past. A good deal of the hiring in the computer industry is managed through headhunters.

Most cities have a great number of personnel agencies handling the local or wider areas. Many of them can be useful in a campaign since they may have local contacts and sources of prospects. The best way to determine which agencies to use is by word of mouth and the yellow pages.

Executive search firms are another source of possible openings. They also obtain a fee for making a match between candidate and employer. However, there are several differences between them and personnel agencies. Search firms usually handle higher-level positions, up to top-officer levels. They often have an exclusive contract to fill a position on a fixed fee or contingency basis. They usually seek out people who are not looking for a job and lure them to consider talking with their clients.

TECHNICAL JOB FAIRS

Technical job fairs bring together in one place many different companies seeking to hire qualified people trained in computer science and other technical and engineering disciplines. Job fairs are usually held at a hotel or other central location in large cities. These events will be well-publicized in newspapers and on radio.

At job fairs, employers set up information displays and company representatives talk informally with interested individuals about their company and its work. Because of the demand in recent years for computer-savvy personnel, these job fairs have become a very popular way for employers and potential employees to find out about each other. While most companies at job fairs are looking for individuals with some work experience, students and recent graduates can still benefit from the opportunity to learn more directly about the computer industry and to meet people who may be of assistance in securing a first job.

ON-LINE JOB RESOURCES

If you are new to the Internet, you might be pleasantly surprised at the amount of job-search information to be found online. One valuable reference book to guide you in your Internet job search is *The Guide to Internet Job Searching,* by Margaret Riley, co-published by the Public Library Association and VGM Career Horizons.

Your Internet account can help you find a job, provide you with vital information about prospective employers, and give you a fast and convenient way to communicate with potential employers. As with all business activities on the Internet, it pays to be careful in using the Internet to look for a job.

The Usenet newsgroups **misc.jobs.offered, misc.jobs.offered.entry** (for entry-level positions), and **misc.jobs.contract** have many listings of jobs at all levels and in many fields, both computer-related and otherwise. They also contain messages offering work-at-home scams, get-rich-quick schemes, and job-seeking services of dubious value. It is generally easy to tell the legitimate job offers from the scams. As a rule of thumb, respond only to offers that list specific skill requirements and contain a verifiable return address. In no circumstances should you ever send money to someone offering a work-at-home business "opportunity."

The DICE bulletin board system (Data Processing Independent Consultant's Exchange) is accessible via direct dial lines in several cities in the United States. It is also accessible via telnet at **dice.com** or IP address **199.190.78.2.** DICE usually has thousands of job listings from all parts of the United States as well as overseas, although more jobs are listed in northern California than in any other area. Many of the jobs are senior level or contract positions. You can use keyword searches to narrow your job search on DICE, and job listings frequently include salary information.

Another on-line resource for job listings is CareerPath.com, an employment service featuring listings from The Boston Globe, Chicago Tribune, Los Angeles Times, New York Times, San Jose Mercury News, and the Washington Post. CareerPath.com is free and can be accessed at **http://www.careerpath.com**.

For general career information and guidance, you can turn to the Career Center, which has been available through America Online since 1989. The Career Center is staffed by professional employment counselors and offers a variety of information services. In addition to group chat sessions, one-on-one career counseling sessions, and information on career development, you can find examples of resumes and job letters, download information about job openings, get information on employment agencies across the United States, learn about employment with the federal government, and learn about other information resources.

Finally, many companies maintain their own Web pages. If you are preparing for an interview, thinking about accepting a job, or just curious about a company, visit its Web site.

JOB APPLICATION LETTERS

The job application letter is a three-to-four paragraph summary of your education and qualifications for employment. It is accompanied by and introduces your resume, which describes your credentials in considerably more detail. Because it is sent with your resume, this letter is different than the campaign letter described above, but uses the same positive techniques.

In the first paragraph of your letter, you should identify the position you are seeking (be specific here) and how you found out about the opening, if it is relevant. You should also add a brief statement of your qualifications for the job.

In the second (and if necessary, third) paragraph of your letter, you describe your education, extracurricular activities, previous work experience, and any special skills or qualifications you may possess. Emphasize the way in which your education and experience increase your potential value to the organization to whom you are applying. You may need to do some homework to find out about that organization to make this information convincing. Remember, too, that concrete examples and details are much more effective than vague generalizations. "My summer and part-time work experience as an operator in my college's Computing Center has made me familiar with the day-to-day operations of a large information center" is much better than "I gained experience working summers."

The closing paragraph of your letter should indicate your willingness to be interviewed. If possible, suggest a specific period of time when you will be available, or let the company know when and how they can most easily reach you to make an appointment. And if you have not mentioned it earlier, this is the place to invite the reader to examine your enclosed resume.

You can find examples of job letters and resumes on America Online's Career Center. Many books are also available on this topic. Check your local bookstore for help.

Throughout your letter of application, maintain a confident and professional tone. While all job letters are, in the final analysis, sales pitches, avoid a bragging or aggressive tone. At the same time, highlight your accomplishments. Avoid humble or overly effusive language.

You should generally allow two to three weeks' response time from the date the company can be expected to have received your job letter and resume. After that time, a follow-up telephone call is appropriate. Simply state that you have submitted your resume and are calling to check on the status of your application.

RESUMES

Resumes come in many styles, including:

Chronological. The chronological resume lists your education and work experience, starting with your most recent position and working back in time. For each job, you include your title, dates of employment, employer's name, and a description of your responsibilities and duties and accomplishments. The most common form of resume, the chronological resume, is also the one many college students will use when seeking their first job, especially if they have work experience.

Functional. The functional resume organizes your experience according to your major areas of knowledge or accomplishments, rather than in simple chronological order. Job titles, names of employers, dates of employment, and a description of duties are usually left out. The functional resume emphasizes what you are able to do well: your talents, skills, and abilities. The functional resume is useful if you have done well in school but do not have any work experience. It is also a good style for those making a career change.

Targeted. The targeted resume is a hybrid form that includes information found in both the chronological and the functional resume—information about your education, work experience, and skills. It also includes the title or a description of the position you are seeking, and lists those skills that support your interest in that objective.

Regardless of the style of resume you use, you will want to cover the following information:

- *Your name, address, and phone number.* This information should be placed conspicuously at the top of the page and can serve as a heading. There is no need to include the word "resume," as this will be obvious to the reader. If you are still in school but are nearing graduation (or if for other reasons you include two addresses), make it clear to the reader to which address he or she should respond. You can label one "School Address," the other "Permanent Address," or specify "Address Until (date)" and "Address After (date)."
- *Career Objective.* In this section, describe the type of position you are seeking. Be specific: "A position as an applications programmer that uses my knowledge of accounting" is far more effective than "Seeking an entry-level position in computing."

    You can omit an objective section but, if well-written and precise, its inclusion projects an image of a knowledgeable professional. Sometimes, especially in the case of graduate students, this section is titled "Interests" and describes areas in which the job candidate wishes to concentrate.

- *Education.* Your degree (or degrees, if you have attended graduate school), major, college or university, and date of graduation are listed in this section, together with information on your minor or field of specialization. Other information may also be included. You may (and sometimes should) include a list of courses you have taken that are related to the position for which you are applying. If your grade point average is 3.0 or better, include this fact, as well as any honors, achievements, or awards. And if you have paid for part or all of your education, say so. Companies are impressed with job applicants who demonstrate such responsibility and motivation. Sometimes extracurricular activities will be included in this section, sometimes placed under a separate heading.
- *Work Experience.* List the company, location, dates, and position of any work experience. Stress your responsibilities, the skills each job demanded, and the qualifications you gained from working. If you have held a number of diverse summer and part-time jobs, do not list every one. Describe them under a single, general heading. Highlight any work experience directly relevant to your career objective.
- *Computer Languages and Equipment Experience.* Most employers will want to know the programming languages and development tools you have used as well as the equipment and systems with which you are familiar.
- *Professional Affiliations and Activities.* Your membership in professional organizations testifies to your commitment to computers and computing. List those organizations to which you belong and any other relevant professional activities. Sometimes, especially if you have been active in a student chapter of a professional group, you can combine this section with a description of your other extracurricular activities.
- *Other Facts.* While it is certainly true that your degree and work experience will go a long way toward securing your employment, the more your resume reflects a well-rounded, interesting individual, the more arresting it will be. Sometimes this category is called "Personal" or "Personal Facts," or simply "Other." It may include, variously, your date (and place) of birth; your hobbies, interests, or

special or unique qualifications. Do you have a pilot's license? Do you like to travel, ski, or garden? Do you speak a foreign language, or have you lived abroad? These and other facts can be listed here. Married males may mention their marital status; others should not. You can also use this section to specify your geographical preference and willingness to relocate or travel. Information on your citizenship, military experience, and security clearances should also be provided. Many projects in the computer and other high technology industries are funded, directly or indirectly, by the U.S. government. Individuals engaged in these projects may be required to hold U.S. citizenship and/or security clearances.

- *References.* At the bottom of your resume, you can indicate your willingness to supply references that will attest to your professional and personal qualifications. It is usually best to simply say that "References will be provided on request." A "References" section need not be included on a resume. Obviously, you will be expected to provide references if asked.

You need to line up individuals willing to provide recommendations for you well in advance of your job search. Professors and previous employers will be your best sources of professional references. Personal or character references can be provided by anyone who has known you well and can speak for your integrity and other character traits. Family friends, physicians, or religious leaders are likely choices. It is not a good idea, though, to ask fellow students for such references. Choose individuals whose opinion will have some weight and credibility with employers.

Always ask an individual if he or she feels able to recommend you. If someone feels able to provide only a lukewarm or very general recommendation, it is better to look elsewhere. When someone does agree to recommend you, give him or her a copy of your resume. Sit down and talk with the person about your background and career goals. The more your references know about your work, your ambitions, and the job you are applying for, the more effective their recommendations will be.

Two model resumes are reproduced on the following pages. These resumes show the qualifications of recent graduates of the same computer science undergraduate program seeking employment in computing. The first shows an individual with a technical emphasis, the second portrays someone with business skills and an interest in applications programming.

PREPARING FOR A JOB INTERVIEW

It is extremely important to prepare for a job interview by finding out as much as possible about the company with whom you will be talking. A trip to the library can help. You might begin by looking up the company in *Standard and Poor's Register of Corporation Executives* or *Dunn and Bradstreet's Million Dollar Directory*. These two publications give general information about larger U.S. corporations. If the company is publicly traded, more specialized information can be found in the quarterly and annual reports to stockholders. These reports may be available in your campus library or can be obtained by writing directly to the company. Some knowledge of a company's financial situation will be especially important to job candidates emphasizing business applications of computers.

Newspaper and magazine articles give the most recent information about how and what a company is doing and are good for finding out about technical developments as well as company problems. A simple way to find out what has been published about a company is to look it up in *Business Periodicals Index,* the *F&S Index,* or the index to the *Wall Street Journal.* You can also look up companies on the Internet and various on-line services. If the company has a web page, make sure you visit it before your interview.

Popular publications such as *Business Week* and *PC Magazine* can keep you up-to-date on overall trends and advances in the computer industry. Most large corporations prepare their own recruiting literature to inform applicants about their work. These publications may be on file in your college placement office.

What kinds of questions can you expect an interviewer to ask? Most interviewers will want to know about your academic background: which courses you enjoyed, which you did not like, and how your education

R. H. Sturtevant
333 Inverness Drive
Waco, Texas 76710
(817) 555-5555

OBJECTIVE: Seeking a challenging position as a SYSTEMS PROGRAMMER/ANALYST in the computer or telecommunications industry.

EDUCATION: B.S., Computer Science, Texas A&M University, College Station, Texas, May, 1995. Minor field of study in Industrial Engineering. GPA: 3.2. GPA in major: 3.5

Programming Projects: a trace program written in OS ALP and a control program linking several IBM PS/2 computers to form a pseudo-minicomputer.

PROGRAMMING LANGUAGES: Assembly (ALP), FORTRAN, PL/1, object-oriented C, Pascal, and SCO Unix.

EQUIPMENT EXPERIENCE: AMDAHL 470 V6 and V7B with IBM MVS/JES3 Operating System; DATA GENERAL M10000 with AOS/VS Operating System; IBM PS/2 personal computers; Apple Macintosh.

WORK EXPERIENCE: KWTX-TV, Waco, Texas. Worked as Program Director, On-Air Director, and Floor Director. Responsibilities included running commercials and other television network "cut-ins," organizing local television productions, supervising technical staff. Able to work successfully under tight time schedules. Employed 1988–91.

KBTX-TV, Bryan, Texas. Worked part-time while in college to partially defray educational expenses. Duties essentially identical to those performed at KWTX. Employed 1992–94.

OTHER FACTS: Member, IEEE Computer Society, Association for Computing Machinery. Active in student chapters in ACM. Enjoy flying, backpacking, snow skiing, racquetball, and classical music. Prefer position in Texas or the Southwest.

REFERENCES: Available on request from Placement Center, J. Earl Rudder Conference Tower, Texas A&M University, College Station, Texas 77843.

Jeffery A. Jekel
P.O. Box 99999
College Station, Texas 77844
(409) 555-5555

objective	Seeking a position as an applications programmer/analyst that uses my accounting skills in a business data processing environment.
education	B.S., Computer Science, Texas A&M University, College Station, Texas, May, 1995. Successfully completed eighteen hours of Accounting. Maintained a 3.43 grade point average in major field of study. Earned 25% of educational expenses.
programming languages	Programming coursework emphasized structured programming techniques. Languages include IBM 360/370 Assembler, COBOL, PL/1, PASCAL, BASIC, APL.
equipment experience	AMDAHL 470 V6 and V7B with IBM MVS/JES3 Input Service; Data General MV800 with AOS/VS Operating System; Apple, Radio Shack, and Texas Instruments microcomputers.
professional affiliations & extracurricular activities	Member of Association for Computing Machinery, IEEE Computer Society, and Data Processing Management Association. Participated in intramural sports: volleyball, racquetball, squash.
work experience 1990–95	Worked during summers and holidays for Pizza Hut, Incorporated, in Kingsville, Texas. Promoted to shift leader and given responsibility for all aspects of restaurant operations in manager's absence.
other information	Interests include beekeeping, organic gardening, reading, travel. Willing to relocate and to retrain to meet company needs.
references	References furnished on request.

Finding a Job 115

prepares you for the opportunities their organization offers. They will ask you about your extracurricular activities, interests, and work experience. You may be asked to identify your strengths and accomplishments—and your weaknesses. Interviewers look for candidates with clear career goals. The more you know about the kind of work you want to do in the computer field, the better you will be able to respond to questions about your career direction. And many interviewers will want to know where, based on what you know about their operations, you see yourself most effectively working. Again, note that the best-prepared job candidate has done his or her homework on the company.

Some other general guidelines to help you interview successfully include:

- Be punctual. Be on time—or better, arrive a few minutes early so you can gather your thoughts and catch your breath before the interview begins.
- Dress professionally. Whether you like it or not, visual impressions are important. Come with extra copies of your resume. You may also want to carry a professional-looking briefcase or binder. While you may find that in some computer companies jeans and hiking boots are the standard attire, wait until you have a job to adopt less conservative dress. Even then, strive to project an image of professionalism. Acceptable on-the-job dress for software professionals differs by geographic region and by type of job. On the West Coast, software developers working for vendors routinely wear jeans, shorts, and t-shirts. Software developers at large companies elsewhere often—but not always—get away with wearing their most comfortable clothes. IS professionals tend to dress more conservatively, although again, on the West Coast, programmers working for even the largest corporations are more causal than elsewhere. Once you have a job, do not buy a new wardrobe for work until you see how others dress. But remember: clean clothes (no matter how casual) and a well-groomed appearance will contribute to an image of professional competence.
- Be personable. Maintain good eye contact, shake hands firmly, smile. Be positive, confident, poised, enthusiastic. Listen actively

to the interviewer's questions. A successful interview is a dialogue, not an interrogation.
- Ask questions. The interview is your chance to learn about the employment and advancement opportunities, working conditions, special programs, benefits, and general atmosphere in which you will be working. Your research on the company will help you prepare specific questions for the interviewer. Asking informed questions will also demonstrate your interest in the company.

Be sure to obtain the interviewer's name, title, and company address. Within a day or two of your interview, write a short follow-up letter, thanking the interviewer for taking time to talk to you about the company. You might point out a feature of working with that company that particularly interests you, and you should express your continuing interest in employment.

Most interviewers will tell you when you can expect to hear from them. If they do not, be sure to ask them for a date. You can do this gracefully by pointing out that you are interviewing with other companies and would like to know when you can expect their decision to be made.

In general, approach the interview and your overall search for employment with these thoughts in mind:

- Employers hire *people,* not degrees.
- Employers prefer people who set clear career objectives.
- Assuming your education and skills are appropriate, the most important aspect of an interview or site visit is the chance for both you and your respective employer to see how you "fit" with one another. This concept of "fit" or suitable match is crucial to your future success at a given company.

SOME PRACTICAL SUGGESTIONS

Experienced job hunters know that the search for employment can itself become a nearly full-time job. Finding a job takes research skills, organization, and persistence, even in the computer field where so many opportunities exist. Plan to devote a considerable amount of time and energy to your job search. If you are still in school, you may want to plan your last semester so that you have enough time to look for employment without sacrificing your academic standing.

Some very practical suggestions:

- Buy yourself a personal organizer. Write down appointments, interviews, and dates you can expect to hear from employers. Also record all telephone conversations and the dates you send out letters and resumes. You can also use your PC and applications like Starfish's Sidekick to help keep track of this process.
- Keep copies of all correspondence with employers. You may need to refer to this correspondence.
- Be persistent and follow through on all leads. If you send out a job letter and do not receive a response within two to three weeks, write or telephone the employer to inquire about your status. If an interviewer says that you will hear from them in three weeks and you do not, make a phone call. Your papers may have been lost in the shuffle.
- Do not take rejection personally. Your qualifications and your style will not suit the hiring needs (or styles) of all employers. This does not make you any less qualified.

EVALUATING EMPLOYMENT OFFERS

When you receive an offer of employment, there are a number of factors you should consider before accepting the job, especially if you are trying to choose among more than one offer. Some things to think about include:

Benefits. It may seem strange to be thinking about retirement when you have not yet started your first job. But retirement, life, health, and dental insurance, disability coverage, and investment plans are no less a part of your total salary than is your basic wage. Companies also vary in their vacation, holiday, personal day, and sick day allocations.

Other specific benefits to consider are 401K and employee stock purchase plans, profit sharing, and employee incentive options. A 401K plan allows you to save a percentage of your income before taxes, thus reducing your overall taxable income. The 401K plan is meant to be a savings plan for retirement. However, you can borrow against it or take out money in certain cases: for instance, to buy a house or in the case of a major illness in your family. Your 401K plan can be transferred when you change employers. Many employers match a certain portion of your 401K contribution. This can prove to be a very attractive savings plan.

Employee stock purchase plans allow you to purchase shares of your company's stock at a discount, usually at the lower of the beginning and ending price during a designated period. Stock plans encourage employees to invest in their own future. If the company does well, the employee, as a shareholder, also benefits.

Some companies in the computer industry also have profit sharing plans, letting all workers share in a percentage of profits. Employee incentive options reward valuable employees by giving them an opportunity to purchase blocks of stock at a considerable discount. As an entry-level employee, you should not expect to be recruited with promises of options. As you progress in your career, however, it will be something to ask about, especially when considering employment with a small or start-up company.

Finally, many companies offer tuition reimbursement programs to their employees. Education is expensive, so tuition reimbursement can be a very attractive benefit. Many people in the computer industry pursue their master's degree in a part-time program or simply take courses at company expense to keep up-to-date while working full-time.

You may find it difficult to read through the description of employee benefits, which may be written in opaque and legalistic language. Try to make a list of benefits provided by the employer and calculate their worth. In comparing two employers, one offering a higher salary, the other better benefits, subtract the value of those benefits from the more attractive salary to see what you really will be making.

Geographical location. The cost of living in different parts of the country varies dramatically. A high salary for Dallas or Atlanta may not go very far in San Francisco or Boston. You need to decide how important living in a particular city, state, or region is to you. You may also need to accommodate your geographical preferences to the realities of the job market. Are you more concerned with what you do or where you do it?

Opportunities for advancement. Will a position allow you to grow and develop professionally? What opportunities will you have to move upward and outward in the organization? Will working for this employer help you to achieve your career goals? What is the employer's policy regarding promotions?

Employment security. A young, expanding company may offer opportunities for rapid advancement. At the same time, it may be financially less stable. Do you seek the security of an established company, or are you attracted by the advantages and risks of a more volatile organization?

Company culture. Some companies are conservative in appearance, attitude, and procedures. Some foster competitive, fast-paced, intense working conditions; others are more measured, relaxed, or stratified. Try to match your own characteristics to the style of an organization. Select the employer with whom you will feel most comfortable.

INTANGIBLE JOB SATISFACTIONS

When evaluating possible career directions or prospective employers, remember to consider the intangible satisfactions as well as the salaries and benefits that you can anticipate. These intangible rewards vary, of course, because of the many different types of jobs within the software industry. Also, different people will find satisfaction in different aspects of a given job.

Some of the kinds of satisfaction that professionals in the field of software have found include:

- A good feeling at being part of a field that is in the forefront of innovation and change in business, government, and our individual daily lives
- The enjoyment of seeing specific beneficial results from your individual work effort, such as an easier system, lower costs, better quality, or customer satisfaction
- Gratification at being part of a team, working with people you like
- Contentment with a programming or research position where you find and resolve problems

- Satisfaction gained from being a part of a project with a beginning and end, of successfully bringing a product to market or seeing your software deployed throughout your company
- The feeling of being respected in playing an advisory or supportive role and for sometimes being considered an expert

People like Bill Gates, the founder of Microsoft, Steve Jobs, the cofounder of Apple and NeXT, and Phillippe Kahn, the founder of Borland and now the head of Starfish Software still display excitement and pride when showcasing the latest of their companies' products.

Realistically, there will be times when you will be frustrated, dissatisfied, or simply tired of working on a particular project. In this, software is no different than any other line of work. You may not like your manager, you may find yourself in a position with little advancement potential, or you may feel under-appreciated. When you find yourself in this position, you can take heart from Scott Adams's cartoon strip, "Dilbert," a satiric look at the foibles of high-tech employment. Realize your situation is not unique. Then try to address the problems in a positive fashion. And if you are truly unable to rectify the situation, then move on to greener pastures.

CHAPTER 8

EMPLOYMENT OUTLOOK: SHAPING YOUR CAREER

In this chapter we will look at a number of factors that will be important to you as you shape a career as a computer professional. We will look at geographical distribution and trends in the demand for software professionals, entry-level salaries, your possible career path, and the opportunities for advancement you can expect. Finally, we will touch briefly on some of the major technical and business directions that will be a factor in employment over the next several years.

GEOGRAPHICAL DISTRIBUTION

At the dawn of the personal computer revolution in the early 1980s, most computer-related employment was concentrated in major metropolitan areas where companies using large, general-purpose mainframe computers were located. Today, the proliferation of personal computers and advances in communications—plus the computerization of nearly every kind of job—means that you can live almost anywhere and still work in the computer field.

A large number of positions are still located in major cities. New York, Boston, Los Angeles, San Francisco, and Dallas-Ft. Worth have large concentrations of computer professionals employed in a variety of industries.

The route from Washington, D.C. to Frederick, Maryland, has become an increasingly important center of employment because of its proximity to federal government agencies. The federal government is itself a major employer of computer professionals in every department. Also, many computer companies maintain sales and marketing offices in the Washington, D.C. area that focus on selling to the federal government.

While hardware and software vendors of varying sizes are located in regions all over the United States, job opportunities are still clustered on the West and East coasts. California's Silicon Valley—an area that includes San Jose, Sunnyvale, Cupertino, and neighboring cities—still accounts for much of the innovation in microprocessor technology, hardware, and software. Larger companies, such as Hewlett Packard, Apple, and Oracle, are found alongside innumerable smaller companies and start-ups.

The San Francisco Bay area is also a center for multimedia development, including multimedia title development, games, and advanced computer graphics used in film and video. It is home to multimedia innovators like Silicon Graphics, Macromedia, and Industrial Light and Magic, the company responsible for countless special effects in many of your favorite movies.

San Francisco and Los Angeles are centers for banking and financial services, as well as manufacturing and transportation. Employment opportunities abound for information systems professionals in both of these cities. Additionally, aerospace and defense contractors in Southern California continue to hire software and systems professionals, despite recent cutbacks in the federal defense budget.

Boston and its surrounding suburbs are also home to a number of leading hardware and software vendors. Companies such as Digital Equipment Corp., Lotus (an IBM subsidiary), and Data General have spun off a number of other high-tech companies. The Greater Boston area is also a center of financial services and insurance. Skilled information systems professionals are always in demand in these industries.

New York City is another major center of employment for information systems professionals. Indeed, today's global financial market is only possible because of innovative technology developed for use by

Wall Street brokerages and major international banks headquartered in New York. Most positions with computer manufacturers in New York will be in sales and support.

Other areas of the United States with a higher-than-average concentration of hardware and software vendors include Texas, the Pacific Northwest, and Florida. In Texas, "Silicon Gulch" is home to companies like Compaq, Dell, and Texas Instruments. Dallas and Houston also offer opportunities for systems professionals in oil and gas transportation, and banking industries.

Microsoft, in Redmond, Washington, has been a major factor in the growth of the Pacific Northwest as a center for hardware and software development, together with other companies like Adobe in Seattle and Intel and Tektronix in the Portland area.

You need not live in a major metropolitan area to enjoy a successful career in computers. Every region of the United States offers job opportunities. In information processing and business applications, opportunities exist in banking, insurance, financial services, manufacturing, health care, education, and government. In fact, the major growth segment for sales of computer hardware and software in recent years has been to small businesses. Furthermore, more and more people are working from home offices. Small businesses, home office workers, and consumers all will require varying levels of computer services.

Telecommuting will have a major influence on expanding the limits of geography for people working with computers. Advances in telecommunications and decreases in the cost of communications mean that more and more software developers can work from home. For instance, Aspect Telecommunications in San Jose, California has made it possible for one of their senior developers to telecommute from his home in the mountains of Colorado. McGraw-Hill Home Interactive is building teams of software developers who work offsite and communicate electronically. Increasingly, telecommuting will become commonplace for many software professionals.

The bottom line: as a software professional, you enjoy more freedom of choice in where you work than do professionals in many other industries.

DEMAND

The demand for software professionals is expected to continue to grow much faster than average through the year 2005, according to the Bureau of Labor Statistics. The rate of growth, however, will be somewhat slower than it was during the 1970s and 1980s, as the computer industry has matured to become one of the largest American industries.

Overall employment in business services industries is expected to grow from 5.3 million jobs in 1992 (the most recent year for which numbers are available) to 8.3 million in 2005. Within the business services industries, two areas are expected to see the fastest growth: personnel supply services (primarily, temporary help agencies) and computer and data processing services. The rapid growth in the demand for computer and data processing services is being fueled by advances in technology, world-wide trends towards factory and office automation, and increases in demand from business firms, government agencies, and the small-business and consumer markets.

Overall growth in professional specialty occupations (under which the Bureau of Labor classifies computer professionals) is expected to increase by 37 percent from 1992 to 2005, from 16.6 to 22.8 million jobs. For example, in 1992 there were about 666,000 systems analyst positions in the United States; by 2005, there will be 737,000 more openings than in 1992. Computer scientists, engineers, and systems analysts (as well as operations research analysts) will be among the fastest growing professional specialty occupations through at least 2005. In addition, tens of thousands of job openings will occur annually as a result of the need to replace those workers who move into managerial positions or other occupations.

What this means is that those with a college degree in computer science or related field should enjoy excellent employment prospects. In large part, this is due to the fact that the number of college graduates with a degree in computer science has not kept pace with employers' needs. Even as demand has increased, the number of college degrees awarded in computer science has been falling since the mid-1980s. In 1992–93, only 24,200 degrees were awarded, compared with 41,889 in 1985–86. As a consequence, even college graduates with non-computer science degrees, but who have had a number of courses in programming, systems analysis, or information processing—and some practical job experience—should be able to find jobs as systems analysts. Moreover, new fields such as multimedia offer opportunities to those who couple computer skills with creative design or production.

One trend may be especially appealing to people for whom job flexibility and continual new challenges is important: contracting. Increasingly, computer vendors and other businesses hire programmers on a contract basis for a single project. These projects may last from a few months to a year or more. Rather than having to lay off employees at the end of the project, employers are turning to contract workers to meet their programming needs. In 1995, approximately one in five (or close to 18 percent) of the programmers working in California's Silicon Valley were contract workers. The Bureau of Labor expects the number of contract workers in this field to increase as more companies outsource computer operations (discussed in the following section) or form teams for a specific project that disband once the project is completed.

Contractors are usually paid on an hourly basis. They often make more per hour than full-time employees. However, they generally do not receive the additional benefits—vacation, sick days, health and other insurance, investment and retirement accounts—that full-time employees enjoy.

Few people are hired as contractors for development work right out of school. Contractors are specialists and must come prepared with the skills needed for the project in question. With a few years' experience, though, many people enjoy the freedom that contracting affords, which allows them to spend more time with their children, to travel, or simply to move on to a new project.

TRENDS THAT MAY AFFECT DEMAND

While the overall demand for software professionals is expected to expand rapidly over the next several years, demand for some technical skills will inevitably diminish. The proliferation of the networked personal computer, combined with the growing use of smaller, more powerful computers as servers, has meant than many businesses are reducing their reliance on the traditional large mainframe computer. While mainframe computers will persist, the role these machines play in a company's information systems architecture is already changing. Primary business applications that once were run on these "host" machines are now distributed on smaller computers in the trend to downsize computer operations. At the same time, the vast amount of data that today's information-intensive business operations require means that the mainframe computer plays a key role in storing vital company information. Therefore, while demand for traditional mainframe programmers will decline, demand for skills in mainframe computers will persist, although at a lower level than in previous years.

The changing role of the mainframe computer is only one example of the ways in which technological and business changes affect demand for programmers and systems analysts. For example, at one time many industry analysts expected that IBM's OS/2 operating system and its user interface (the Presentation Manager) would be widely adopted by businesses. At the time, skilled OS/2 programmers could command higher-than-average salaries. In the mid-1990s, OS/2 was used on only a fraction of computers and demand was highest for programmers skilled in Microsoft's Windows.

The lesson to be learned from this is that the demand for specific technical skills changes rapidly in the computer systems field. In order to stay competitive, you need to stay on top of market trends and keep your own skills in line with those trends.

In addition to changing trends in technology, two other factors may affect the demand for software professionals over the next few years: outsourcing and globalization. Outsourcing is the subcontracting of systems and data processing design, implementation, and maintenance to outside service organizations. Companies outsource some or all of their information systems work because they expect that it will cost less and free management to focus more on its own products and services. This trend is reducing the number of information systems specialists needed within individual companies. On the other hand, it increases employment opportunities with service organizations, consulting organizations, and systems integrators.

A second trend that will affect employment in the coming years is the globalization of business. While many computer vendors are expanding their overseas market share, the globalization of business means many jobs that once might have been performed in the United States can now be done more economically in other countries. For years, companies like American Airlines and CitiCorp have sent paper records overseas on overnight flights to Jamaica, the Philippines, or the Dominican Republic to be keyed into computer systems by lower-paid data entry workers. Advances in telecommunications has made it even easier for companies to set up global networks and to move data entry and manufacturing jobs offshore. According to a 1995 article in *Business Week,* more and more high-tech jobs, including computer design and development, are following data-entry and manufacturing jobs overseas. For example, Silicon Graphics has established a joint venture in Bangalore (India's answer to Silicon Valley), where software developers earn $300 a month developing advanced imaging software. In Taiwan, engineers who would earn up to $100,000 a year in the United States earn $25,000; in India or China, that same engineer might make $10,000 a year at best. The same communications technology that lets U.S. software developers telecommute from the Rockies to San Jose also lets programmers in Bangalore "telecommute" to San Jose.

It is still too early to say what effect that globalization will have on salary and overall demand for software professionals in the United States. Nevertheless, it is important to keep in mind that, in the words of Edith Holleman, counsel to the U.S. House of Representatives' Science, Space and Technology Committee, high-tech jobs "are not reserved for you in the First World." All the more reason to maintain and refresh your technical skills throughout your career.

SALARY STATISTICS

The most recent U.S. government figures available indicate that median earnings for programmers working full-time in 1992 were about $35,600, with the lowest 10 percent earning less than $19,700 and the

Representative Vertical Career Paths in Computer Vendor Organizations

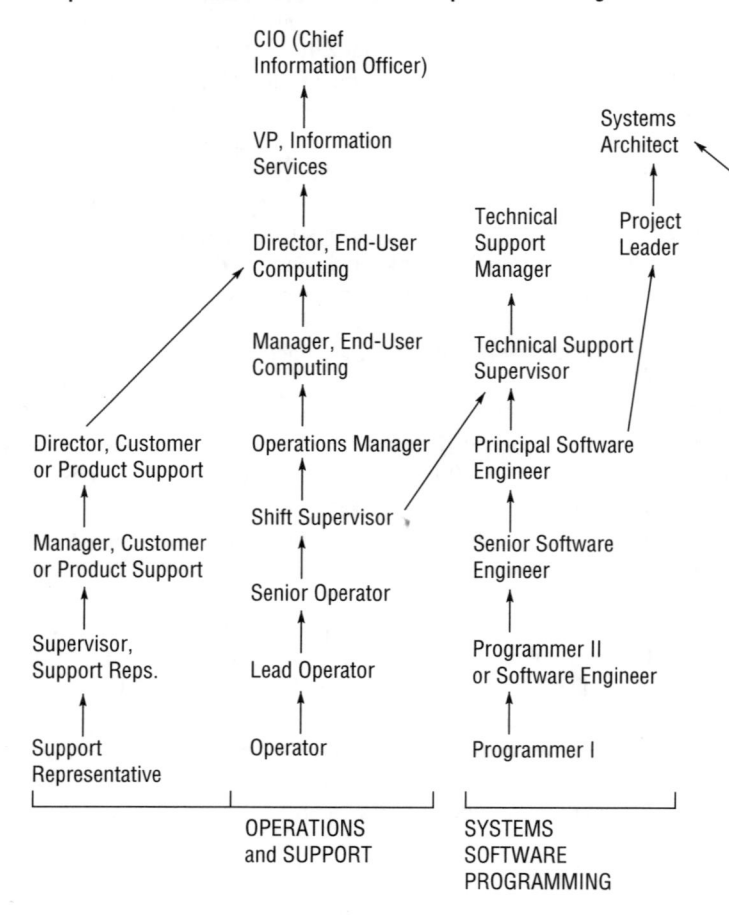

```
                              CIO (Chief
                              Information Officer)
                                    ↑
                                                        Systems
                              VP, Information           Architect ←
                              Services                      ↑
                                    ↑                       |
                                                Technical   Project
                              Director, End-User  Support   Leader
                            ↗ Computing         Manager       ↑
                                    ↑              ↑
                              Manager, End-User  Technical Support
                              Computing         Supervisor
                                    ↑              ↑
    Director, Customer        Operations Manager  Principal Software
    or Product Support              ↑            Engineer
          ↑                   Shift Supervisor       ↑
    Manager, Customer               ↑            Senior Software
    or Product Support                           Engineer
          ↑                   Senior Operator        ↑
    Supervisor,                     ↑            Programmer II
    Support Reps.             Lead Operator      or Software Engineer
          ↑                         ↑                  ↑
    Support                   Operator            Programmer I
    Representative
    └─────────────────────────────────┘    └─────────────────────┘
                              OPERATIONS           SYSTEMS
                              and SUPPORT          SOFTWARE
                                                   PROGRAMMING
```

Employment Outlook: Shaping Your Career 129

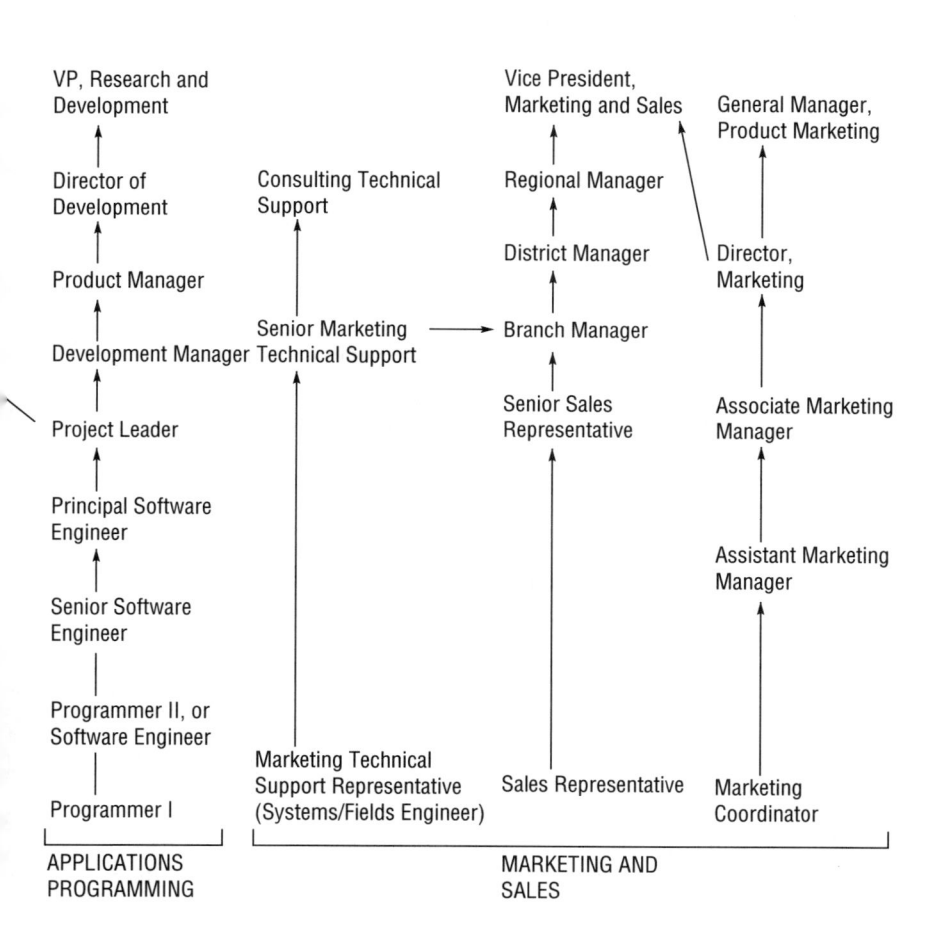

```
VP, Research and              Vice President,
Development                   Marketing and Sales      General Manager,
    ↑                              ↑                   Product Marketing
Director of              Consulting Technical          ↑
Development              Support                  Regional Manager
    ↑                         ↑                        ↑
Product Manager                               District Manager    Director,
    ↑                                              ↑              Marketing
Development Manager      Senior Marketing    → Branch Manager     ↑
    ↑                    Technical Support         ↑
Project Leader                                Senior Sales        Associate Marketing
    ↑                         ↑               Representative      Manager
Principal Software                                 ↑                   ↑
Engineer
    ↑                                                             Assistant Marketing
Senior Software                                                   Manager
Engineer                                                               ↑
    │
Programmer II, or
Software Engineer
    │
Programmer I           Marketing Technical                        Marketing
                       Support Representative  Sales Representative  Coordinator
                       (Systems/Fields Engineer)
APPLICATIONS           
PROGRAMMING                        MARKETING AND
                                   SALES
```

highest 10 percent earning more than $58,000. In general, systems programmers earned more than application programmers.

The median figure for systems analysts in 1992 was somewhat higher at $42,100; at least half of all systems analysts made between $32,000 and $52,200. Ten percent made more than $65,500.

As you can see, computer professionals are well-rewarded financially for their work. An entry-level programmer or software engineer in 1995 could expect to make at least $30,000 to $32,000, and perhaps as much as $39,000 to $45,000, depending on skills and previous work experience. (Remember the advice from our profiled professionals in chapter 5 on the importance of work experience *before* you graduate.)

Entry-level earnings in the federal government and in education tend to be somewhat lower than salaries than in business and the computer industry. However, many of those who work in government and education do so for rewards that are not just monetary. Do not rule out opportunities in these sectors.

CAREER PATHS

Almost without exception, your first position upon graduation will be as a programmer, junior programmer, or quality assurance engineer. From this point, your advancement will depend on your abilities and interests, your initiative, and the career goals you set for yourself.

Two paths of advancement are open to you: a technical path and a path leading into management. In the past, most promotions led into management positions. A successful individual would move from programmer to project leader and into higher management. This generally meant, though, that as an employee advanced, his or her responsibilities became less technical and more managerial. The result was that people with very good technical qualifications but no interest in management were frustrated by a lack of opportunity.

For the most part, this situation has changed. Companies have made dual-paths of advancement available to their employees. New job titles and responsibilities have been created in the technical domain. An employee can still advance into management. But successive levels of technical promotions have been created, in recognition of the fact that many computer professionals will be happiest and most productive if technical avenues of promotion exist.

Large- and mid-size computer hardware and software vendors offer many opportunities to pursue a technical career path. Large vendors offer additional opportunities for the technical person to move laterally into marketing, sales, or customer support. The diagram on the previous pages shows representative vertical career paths in a large vendor organization like IBM or Hewlett Packard. Remember, too, that U.S. companies increasingly are adopting a project team approach, which means a straight-line vertical career path may become less common in the future. Certainly, if you work for smaller companies or start-ups, you will have opportunities to work in quality assurance and technical support, whether you anticipate them or not.

Within vendor organizations, you can move both vertically and laterally. This means that you might move from a technical position into a position in marketing or technical support, or from one design project to another. Such diversified experience within a single company is a good preparation for advancement into the higher levels of management.

Within end-user organizations, you can move vertically as well as laterally. Until recently, MIS departments were structured like a pyramid, with programmers on the bottom and MIS Directors at the top. Three trends have changed this: 1) the increased use of networked desktop PCs and client-server applications; 2) corporate restructuring that makes individual business units within a company accountable for more decision-making (reducing several layers of management, including IS management), and 3) a move to relocate some information systems staff in individual business units. The growing importance of information technology to large organizations has created a new structure under the authority of the CIO, or "Chief Information Officer." In the financial industry, manufacturing, and among Fortune 1000 companies, the role of the information manager has become increasingly important. As computer technology continues to alter the very structure of large organizations, converting the hierarchical organization of the past into the distributed organization of the future, the computer professional will play a critical part in changing the way we work.

ORGANIZATIONAL STRUCTURE UNDER AUTHORITY OF THE CHIEF INFORMATION OFFICER

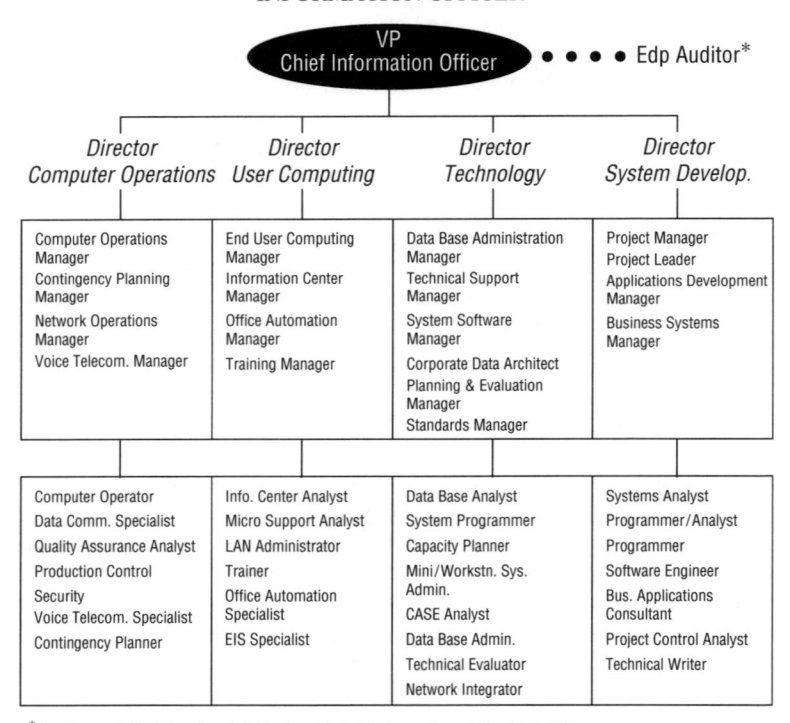

VP Chief Information Officer • • • • Edp Auditor*

Director Computer Operations	Director User Computing	Director Technology	Director System Develop.
Computer Operations Manager Contingency Planning Manager Network Operations Manager Voice Telecom. Manager	End User Computing Manager Information Center Manager Office Automation Manager Training Manager	Data Base Administration Manager Technical Support Manager System Software Manager Corporate Data Architect Planning & Evaluation Manager Standards Manager	Project Manager Project Leader Applications Development Manager Business Systems Manager
Computer Operator Data Comm. Specialist Quality Assurance Analyst Production Control Security Voice Telecom. Specialist Contingency Planner	Info. Center Analyst Micro Support Analyst LAN Administrator Trainer Office Automation Specialist EIS Specialist	Data Base Analyst System Programmer Capacity Planner Mini/Workstn. Sys. Admin. CASE Analyst Data Base Admin. Technical Evaluator Network Integrator	Systems Analyst Programmer/Analyst Programmer Software Engineer Bus. Applications Consultant Project Control Analyst Technical Writer

*Usually reports to CFO or Board of Directors; "dotted line" reporting relationship to CIO.

Source: Source EDP (1995)

SOME EXAMPLES OF TYPICAL CAREER PATHS

This section looks at some examples of typical career paths of individuals who have spent a number of years in computer-related positions. This will give you a small idea of what you can expect in real-life situations. In two examples, the individuals profiled have stayed with a single company throughout their career. Today, this is becoming less and less common. More typically, an individual will work for many employers. In fact, candidates interviewing for technical positions can find themselves at a disadvantage if they have spent more than five to seven years at a given company, as these individuals may not have diversified their technical skills. Note, too, that one example shows a career path that leads to a new, but related, area of business.

Programmer to entrepreneur—fifteen years. This person left law school after the second year, preferring a high-tech to a legal career. Starting as a programmer with a major communications and networking company, he left after four years to work for one of the leading vendors of applications software. He spent three years at this company, where he was promoted to development manager of a small team of developers and successfully shipped one of the first PC-based electronic mail programs. After the product was cancelled (a not uncommon occurrence in the software industry), this individual moved on to become director of development for a small software venture. After one year, he accepted a position as director of development at a mid-sized software company, working on another electronic mail product. In this position he led the development team and was instrumental in determining how the product would function. When his company was acquired by a major hardware vendor, he joined forces with another employee to start a company. Working together, these two individuals developed utilities for administering electronic mail systems. Soon they were able to hire a sales and marketing expert. From this initial three-person team, the company grew in five years to over thirty employees, with growing revenues and solid business plans for continuing success.

Programmer to chief data base architect—eight years. A programmer with a computer science degree desired more technical experience, so, after two years with his first employer, he joined another company as a systems analyst.

After two years as a systems analyst, he was promoted to project manager for a new data base project. Two years later he was asked to become the chief data base architect for another company, a position he has now held for two years and where he earns triple his starting salary.

Salesman to vice-president of data processing—fifteen years. After five years as a salesman with IBM, a Vietnam veteran joined one of his clients, a small manufacturing company, as director of management information, supervising a staff of eight. Three years later, he became manager of systems programming for a large insurance company, directing fifty people. After two years in that position, he was promoted to application development manager with a hundred people within his jurisdiction. He left that position after three years to become the vice-president of data processing for a medium-sized insurance company (at triple his income as a salesman), a position he has now held for two years.

Programmer to consulting firm owner—twelve years. Starting as a programmer with a manufacturing company, a holder of an information science degree left after four years to become a sales consultant for a software company. After two years as a sales consultant, she was promoted to head a staff of twenty people. Then, two years later, she formed her own consulting firm with two other people. This firm has grown during the last four years to have a staff of seventy-five, providing consulting services to its clients. Her salary is now six figures.

Engineer to placement branch manager—twenty-five years. An engineer with both an engineering degree and an MBA spent his first two years as a noncomputer engineer. He then joined IBM as a systems engineer for five years, becoming an IBM salesman for an additional five years. He was asked by one of his clients to be its director of data processing, a position he held for six years. Afterwards he joined a nationwide personnel placement firm, specializing in information systems positions. Five years later he was promoted to manager of one of that firm's offices in a major city, a position he has held for the last two years.

Correspondence clerk to chief information officer—twenty-five years. This head of information systems for a major financial services company has spent his entire career with that company, starting with his first four years as a correspondence clerk. He progressed to a staff and research position for three years, then was promoted to be a project manager in the information services department, a position he held for three years. After that, he became manager of all the programmers for two years and then moved up to be vice-president over various information processing functions for four years. Next, he served as vice-president and assistant to the chief information officer for four years. Five years ago he reached his current position as senior vice-president in charge of all information systems activities.

Programmer to director of information systems—twenty-three years. This person worked for seven years for three different companies while earning a BBA in economics and an MBA in computers methods. He then started as a programmer with a communications company, where he worked for the next twenty-three years until he was released last year due to company reorganization. During those twenty-three years, he held these positions: programmer—two years; manager of systems and programming—two years; director of computer systems for a division—four years; management information systems consultant and director of data base systems for two and five years respectively at corporate headquarters; director of management information systems planning at a division—one year; and finally director of information systems for the same division—seven years. During these years he has done a great deal of teaching, writing, and some consulting and service bureau work on the side. Now in his early fifties, he is expanding these activities into a full-time business.

Mail clerk to senior vice-president of corporate planning—forty years. This person has spent most of his career in data processing, although he began and is ending his career in other areas. Starting as a mail clerk for one year, he was quickly promoted to a senior clerical position for two years and afterwards to a technical specialist job for three years in the financial services company for which he has worked his entire career. He was then made manager of the punched card tabulating department (this person has spent a long time in the computer industry!) with one hundred employees, where he stayed for six years. From there he was promoted to assistant vice-president, supervising over twenty programmers and one hundred data processing people. He remained there for eight more years. All these jobs were in one of the company's divisions. Next he was moved to the headquarters of the parent company and was placed in charge of its data processing, there for ten years as vice-president and for two as assistant to the senior vice-president. Eight years ago he was transferred back to his division as vice-president, managing several of its noncomputer service activities, and five years ago he was promoted to his present position as senior vice-president in charge of corporate planning. He is scheduled to retire soon.

These and many other developments, some not even dreamed of today, will make the field of computing an exciting and rewarding career choice.

A NOTE ABOUT EQUALITY OF OPPORTUNITY

Individuals of any sex, race, creed, or ethnic origin can do well in computer science. Because computer science requires mental, not physical, skills, it can be a good choice for those with physical disabilities. People with limited vision, hearing, and mobility have found successful careers in the computer field.

TECHNOLOGY AND MARKET TRENDS

In the coming years, the following technological advances will be among the factors that drive the computer industry:
- *The continued increase in computing power.* Advances in computer chip manufacture and computer architecture will contribute to the development of ever more powerful computers. The increase in computing power will enable software developers to design new kinds of application programs.
- *Migration of corporate mission-critical applications from mainframe or minicomputers to desktop systems and development of client-server applications.* We can expect to see the relocation of applications from centralized machines to distributed computing resources; the role of the centralized MIS organization will change.
- *Easier-to-use software based on the use of intelligent systems.* Future applications will incorporate human expertise as well as adapt interactively to mesh with the skills and needs of the human user.

- *Hardware and software targeted for specific markets.* Business and personal use software will become increasingly specialized.
- *Networking and telecommunications.* The growth of networking and telecommunications has created new ways for people to work together. Workgroup software will be designed to enable geographically dispersed groups of people to collaborate; telecommunications networks will increasingly provide banking, shopping, and information retrieval services.
- *The growth of the Internet and on-line services.* Networking and telecommunications technologies have fostered an explosion in the use of the Internet and commercial on-line services. In the next few years, much of the excitement in new product development will be in this area.
- *Multimedia.* The CD-ROM storage device, coupled with digital audio and video, have given birth to the rapidly expanding CD-ROM publishing industry. There is a rush to develop educational and entertainment software that can be distributed on CD-ROM. Digital effects developed by companies, such as Industrial Light and Magic, and Pixar, have transformed the way we think about—and create—film and video. Advances in communications bandwidth and compression mean it will soon be practical to distribute interactive multimedia with full production qualities, both on CD-ROM and, more significantly, over the network.
- *The growth in home computing.* In 1995 the computer was a common appliance in nearly four out of ten U.S. households. Historically, much software product development has focused on increasing business productivity. In the future, new ways of enriching everyday life through software will present opportunities that can only be imagined today.

CHAPTER 9
PROFESSIONAL ORGANIZATIONS

Professional and industry organizations provide a forum for the exchange of information and foster the professional development of their members. Most students will join at least one or two professional organizations in college in order to be able to list their membership on their resume.

It is certainly true that potential employers will see membership in professional organizations as an indication of your serious commitment to computer science. But there are many other benefits of membership in these groups. Nearly every professional society listed in the following pages puts out journals, newsletters, or other publications that you receive as part of your membership. Reading these publications can go a long way toward keeping you up-to-date on technological advances. This is especially important because much of what you learn in school will necessarily be a little dated, if only because of the time it takes to publish a textbook.

You can also keep abreast of the latest developments in the industry by attending meetings, seminars, and conferences sponsored by professional groups. You can probably learn more in a single day at an industry trade show such as Comdex, Interop, or PC Expo than you would in several weeks of classroom study. At trade shows you have the opportunity to see what vendors are producing, to hear talks on the latest advances in hardware and software, and to learn about recent trends and the latest products. Additionally, you can meet and talk with people working in the computer industry. These informal contacts can be very useful in giving you a sense of what is really happening in the computer field. Sometimes, such informal contacts can even lead to employment opportunities.

USER GROUPS

Computer user groups are an excellent source of information about computing. PC user groups exist in many parts of the United States. User groups have regular meetings, share software, and are great places to meet other computer users and learn about new products. Many user groups also have their own, local electronic bulletin board or web page.

The Boston Computer Society is one of the largest and oldest of user groups. It supports many special interest groups, invites leading figures in the computer society to address its meetings, and schedules professional development courses each summer. The BCS also has its own bulletin board service, including job postings. You do not need to live in the Boston to realize many of the benefits of membership in the BCS. For information, contact:

The Boston Computer Society
1 Center Plaza
Boston, MA 02108

INDUSTRY ASSOCIATIONS

A very large number of computer-related organizations exist today. Listed here are some of the major organizations in computing, a selection of special interest groups, and groups that many students might like to join. Most of these groups encourage student memberships; some have strong student programs.

AMERICAN SOCIETY FOR INFORMATION SCIENCE (ASIS)
8720 Georgia Avenue
Silver Spring, MD 20910
(301) 495-0900

ASIS is concerned with the ways in which people can use computer-based information systems and the science and technology behind these systems. ASIS is dedicated to creating, organizing, and transmitting knowledge on all aspects of information and its transfers, including what formerly would have been called library science.

There are regional and student chapters of ASIS throughout the United States, Canada, and Europe. ASIS maintains a placement service of available positions in information science.

AMERICAN STATISTICAL ASSOCIATION (ASA)
1429 Duke Street
Alexandria, VA 22314
(703) 684-1221

The oldest constituent organization in AFIPS, the ASA was founded in 1839, long before the advent of electronic computers. The association is made up of over 15,000 persons interested in theoretical and/or applied statistics. In addition to its annual meeting in August, the ASA maintains 75 regional chapters in the United States and Canada. Student memberships are available.

ASSOCIATION FOR COMPUTING MACHINERY (ACM)
1515 Broadway Floor 17
New York, NY 10036
(212) 869-7440

The Association for Computing Machinery stands with the IEEE Computer Society as one of the two major organizations of computer professionals. Founded in 1947, just one year after ENIAC, the first electronic computer, ACM is dedicated to advancing the arts and sciences of computer machinery, techniques, languages, and applications. It encourages the interchange of computer knowledge among professionals and seeks to better inform the general public about computers and computing.

With over 75,000 members and 600 local groups in the United States and abroad, ACM plays an important part in the ongoing education and professional development of computer scientists. More than 30 special interest groups within ACM function as independent, smaller organizations of individuals with a common interest in a wide range of topics of theoretical, practical, or social import. Among ACM's many publications is *Communications of the ACM.*

ACM has an extremely active student program. You will find ACM student chapters at most colleges and universities that have computer science departments. Under the direction of faculty advisors, these chapters sponsor educational and social events. Student contact with members of the computer profession is promoted through the ACM Lectureship Series, which brings outstanding speakers to college campuses.

In addition to chapter activities, ACM holds an annual National Student Programming Contest. Regional winners compete in the finals held at the ACM Computer Science Conference each February. Undergraduate members of ACM can also compete for the George E. Forsythe Award, given annually to the winner of the Student Paper Competition. The winning paper is published in *Communications of the ACM.* Each year, ACM also compiles a guide to graduate assistantships, and awards a prize to the author of an outstanding doctoral dissertation.

You can obtain an up-to-date listing of all ACM student chapters by writing or telephoning the organization's headquarters in New York. Student membership in this organization is strongly recommended.

ASSOCIATION FOR SYSTEMS MANAGEMENT (ASM)
1433 W. Bagley Road
Berea, OH 44017
(216) 243-6900

The ASM is the major organization for systems professionals involved in information systems resource management. The organization encourages the ongoing education of its members through seminars and an annual conference. Although full membership requires a college degree or experience in the field, ASM does offer student memberships.

DATA PROCESSING MANAGEMENT ASSOCIATION (DPMA)
505 Busse Highway
Park Ridge, IL 60068
(708) 825-8124

The Data Processing Management Association serves the information processing and computer management community. Its membership comprises systems analysts, data processing managers, and other information processing personnel. Membership in DPMA is granted through local chapters only. Student chapters are active on many college campuses. The DPMA student chapters are highly career-oriented and provide chances for professional contact.

HEALTHCARE INFORMATION AND MANAGEMENT SYSTEMS SOCIETY
230 E. Ohio Street
Chicago, IL 60611
(312) 664-4467

Members are professionals qualified to analyze, design, and operate hospital information and telecommunications systems.

IEEE COMPUTER SOCIETY (IEEE CS)
1730 Massachusetts Ave., NW
Washington, DC 20036
(202) 371-0101

The IEEE Computer Society, a constituent society of the Institute of Electrical and Electronics Engineers, Inc., ranks with ACM as one of the two major professional organizations for computer scientists and engineers. With over 95,000 members worldwide and over 220 local chapters, the IEEE Computer Society is also the world's largest organization of computer professionals.

The expressed purpose of the Computer Society is to advance the theory, practice, and applications of computer and information processing science and technology. It encourages the ongoing professional education of its members through its sponsorship of conferences, workshops, tutorials, and symposia held each year. The IEEE CS is also a major publisher of magazines, journals, and books on computer science. Its publications include magazines on computer hardware and software design and applications, including the widely read monthly *Computer Magazine,* as well as archival journals reporting the latest advances in computer research. IEEE CS also publishes over 500 books on a wide range of computer-related topics. More than 30 technical committees within IEEE CS unite individuals concerned with many special issues in computer science and technology. Members can also subscribe to an electronic mail service, COMPMAIL, bulletin board, and on-line membership directory.

Because it emphasizes education of computer scientists and engineers, the Computer Society has a strong student program. The society has also been instrumental in designing criteria to improve, standardize, and recognize—by means of ABET accreditation—undergraduate programs in computer-related fields.

INDEPENDENT COMPUTER CONSULTANTS ASSOCIATION
P.O. Box 27412
St. Louis, MO 63131
(314) 830-0750

ICCA members are independent consultants offering software and information management services to businesses and corporations. Local chapters sponsor monthly meetings featuring speakers on issues of current interest and offer opportunities for networking with other consultants.

OPERATIONS RESEARCH SOCIETY OF AMERICA (ORSA)
Mount Royal and Guilford Avenue
Baltimore, MD 21202
(410) 528-4146

ORSA is an organization of operations research professionals, managers, educators, and others interested in scientific methods of decision making that use computers. Areas of interest include optimization, probabilistic models, decision analysis, and game theory. ORSA members are also involved in areas of public concern, such as energy, the environment, urban issues, and defense systems, to which operations research techniques can be applied. ORSA sponsors a visiting lecturers program, offers a placement service, and awards an annual prize for the best paper in the field.

PROFESSIONAL AND TECHNICAL CONSULTANTS
    ASSOCIATION (PATCA)
P.O. Box 4143
Mountain View, CA 94040
(415) 903-8305
Web page: http://www.patca.org:8082/patca/patca_info.html

PATCA is a non-profit organization that brings together a diverse group of consultants who work independently or as members of small consulting firms. It conducts seminars and monthly meetings that keep members up-to-date on the latest technical, legal, and business trends. PATCA also provides a referral service and directory of consultants.

SIMULATION COUNCILS, INC.
4838 Ronson Court
San Diego, CA 92111

SOCIETY FOR COMPUTER SIMULATIONS INTERNATIONAL (SCSI)
P.O. Box 2228
La Jolla, CA 92038
(619) 277-3888

The SCSI is devoted to the use of computers to simulate or model processes, systems, or events. Its members include professionals in science, engineering, mathematics, and computer science. The society publishes a monthly technical journal, *Simulation,* as well as a series of reports on particular applications of simulation techniques.

SOCIETY FOR INDUSTRIAL AND APPLIED MATHEMATICS (SIAM)
3600 Market Street
Philadelphia, PA 19104
(215) 382-9800

SIAM exists to further the applications of mathematics in industry and science and to encourage the exchange of ideas among individuals interested in applied mathematics. It also directs the Institute for Mathematics and Society, which studies the applications of mathematics to major problems of society, and the Institute for the Advancement of Scientific Computing.

SOCIETY OF MANUFACTURING ENGINEERS (SME)
1 SME Drive
P.O. Box 930
Dearborn, MI 48121

The Society of Manufacturing Engineers is an international organization with over 80,000 members around the world. It is vitally concerned with student education and sponsors 197 student chapters. SME is the parent organization of three special interest groups, two of which directly concern computers and computing: the Computer and Automated Systems Association (CASA/SME) and Robotics International (RI/SME).

CASA/SME covers the field of computers and automation in manufacturing. It unites individuals interested in computer-aided design (CAD), computer-aided manufacturing (CAM), and computer-integrated manufacturing (CIM).

Robotics International was founded in 1980 to encourage information exchange in the rapidly emerging field of robotics. RI's bi-monthly magazine, *Robotics Today,* features information on the latest advances in robot technology and the use of robots in manufacturing operations.

SOFTWARE FORUM
P.O. Box 61031
Palo Alto, CA 94306
(415) 854-7219
e-mail: 73771.1176@compuserve.com
Web page: http://www.commerce.net/Software Forum
CompuServe forum: GO SEFNET

If you live in the greater Northern California area, you will want to think about joining the Software Forum (formerly the Software Entrepreneurs' Forum). Founded in 1983, Software Forum is a leading industry association; its mission is to build success for software professionals. Software Forum offers a variety of Special Interest Groups (SIGs), meetings, seminars, and on-line forums on technical, legal, financial, and business issues relating to software. It is a great place to meet other software professionals from all aspects of the software industry. Its growing on-line services include a CompuServe forum and a Web server offering updates on activities, software libraries, and opportunities for electronic networking.

A complete list of titles in our extensive *Opportunities* series

OPPORTUNITIES IN
- Accounting
- Acting
- Advertising
- Aerospace
- Agriculture
- Airline
- Animal & Pet Care
- Architecture
- Automotive Service
- Banking
- Beauty Culture
- Biological Science
- Biotechnology
- Broadcasting
- Building Construction Trades
- Business Communications
- Business Management
- Cable Television
- CAD/CAM
- Carpentry
- Chemistry
- Child Care
- Chiropractic
- Civil Engineering
- Cleaning Service
- Commercial Art & Graphic Design
- Computer Maintenance
- Computer Science
- Computer Systems
- Counseling & Development
- Crafts
- Culinary
- Customer Service
- Data & Word Processing
- Dental Care
- Desktop Publishing
- Direct Marketing
- Drafting
- Electrical Trades
- Electronics
- Energy
- Engineering
- Engineering Technology
- Environmental
- Eye Care
- Farming and Agriculture
- Fashion
- Fast Food
- Federal Government
- Film
- Financial
- Fire Protection Services
- Fitness
- Food Service
- Foreign Language
- Forestry
- Franchising
- Gerontology & Aging Services
- Health & Medical
- Heating, Ventilation, Air Conditioning, and Refrigeration
- High Tech
- Home Economics
- Homecare Services
- Horticulture
- Hospital Administration
- Hotel & Motel
- Human Resources Management
- Information Systems
- Installation & Repair
- Insurance
- Interior Design & Decorating
- International Business
- Journalism
- Laser Technology
- Law
- Law Enforcement & Criminal Justice
- Library & Information Science
- Machine Trades
- Marine & Maritime
- Marketing
- Masonry
- Medical Imaging
- Medical Technology
- Mental Health
- Metalworking
- Military
- Modeling
- Music
- Nonprofit Organizations
- Nursing
- Nutrition
- Occupational Therapy
- Office Occupations
- Optometry
- Paralegal
- Paramedical
- Part-Time & Summer Jobs
- Performing Arts
- Petroleum
- Pharmacy
- Photography
- Physical Therapy
- Physician
- Physician Assistant
- Plastics
- Plumbing & Pipe Fitting
- Postal Service
- Printing
- Property Management
- Psychology
- Public Health
- Public Relations
- Publishing
- Purchasing
- Real Estate
- Recreation & Leisure
- Religious Service
- Research & Development
- Restaurant
- Retailing
- Robotics
- Sales
- Science Technician
- Secretarial
- Social Science
- Social Work
- Special Education
- Speech-Language Pathology
- Sports & Athletics
- Sports Medicine
- State & Local Government
- Teaching
- Teaching English to Speakers of Other Languages
- Technical Writing & Communications
- Telecommunications
- Telemarketing
- Television & Video
- Theatrical Design & Production
- Tool & Die
- Training & Development
- Transportation
- Travel
- Trucking
- Veterinary Medicine
- Visual Arts
- Vocational & Technical
- Warehousing
- Waste Management
- Welding
- Writing
- Your Own Service Business

VGM Career Horizons
a division of *NTC Publishing Group*
4255 West Touhy Avenue
Lincolnwood, Illinois 60646-1975